THE SECOND VICTORY

The Marshall Plan
and the Postwar Revival
of Europe

Robert J. Donovan

Foreword by Clark M. Clifford

Madison Books
New York, Lanham, London

This book is based partly on a narrative text prepared by the author for an exhibition of photographs and documents entitled "The Marshall
Plan: Cooperating to Rebuild Europe," to be on
display in U.S. history museums and presidential
libraries from 1987 to 1989. Both exhibition
and book were commissioned by the German
Marshall Fund of the United States as part of a
tribute to the Marshall Plan on its fortieth
anniversary.

To Claudia and Heidi

Copyright © 1987 by
The German Marshall Fund of the United States

Madison Books
4720 Boston Way
Lanham, MD 20706

3 Henrietta Street
London WC2E 8LU England

Printed in the United States of America

British Cataloging in Publication Information
Available

Library of Congress Cataloging-in-Publication Data

Donovan, Robert J.
    The second victory.

    Bibliography: p.
    Includes index.
    1. Marshall Plan.   2. Economic assistance, American—
Europe.   3. Europe—Economic conditions—1945-
I. Title.
HC240.D65 1987   338.91'73'04   ʌ87-24021
ISBN 0-8191-6498-4 (alk. paper)

CONTENTS

PREFACE

FORTY YEARS or so ago, depending on how the origin is reckoned, the United States undertook the boldest, most successful, and certainly most expensive foreign policy initiative ever attempted in peacetime—the Marshall Plan, officially the European Recovery Program. On June 5, 1947, Secretary of State George C. Marshall broached the proposal in his commencement address at Harvard University. On April 3, 1948, President Harry S Truman signed the Foreign Assistance Act, embodying the Marshall Plan. "Few presidents," he said in a statement, "have had the opportunity to sign legislation of such importance. . . . This measure is America's answer to the challenge facing the free world today."

Fueled by billions of American dollars, it was an economic program with the political end of stabilizing and strengthening Western Europe through revival of its war-damaged economy. In the process the program played a principal role in the greatest event in postwar Europe, the birth of the Federal Republic of Germany, allied with the West. In sum, the Marshall Plan became part of the fabric of European history after 1948 and all the more significant in that it was a cooperative undertaking by Americans and Europeans.

This book is an outgrowth of extensive activities sponsored by the German Marshall Fund of the United States, an independent American foundation in Washington, D.C., to commemorate the fortieth anniversary of the European Recovery Program. The activities, climaxing in an international conference in the Reichstag in Berlin in June 1987, included a traveling exhibition of Marshall Plan photographs and documents. In the next two years this exhibition will appear in a number of cities in the United States and Europe.

The author of this book was the exhibition curator. In 1948 as a correspondent for the *New York Herald Tribune* he covered all the congressional hearings and floor debates on Marshall Plan legislation. He has written extensively on postwar United States foreign policy, particularly in his recent two volumes on the Truman presidency.

The German Marshall Fund, of which Frank E. Loy is president, was established in 1972 by a gift from the people of the Federal Republic of Germany as a memorial to Marshall Plan aid, and to help maintain good relations between the United States and Western Europe. Elizabeth McPherson, the Fund's communications director, edited this book. Both exhibition and book were designed by Kevin Osborn and Anne-Catherine Fallen of Research & Design Associates of Arlington, Virginia.

FOREWORD

THE COMMEMORATION of the fortieth anniversary of the Marshall Plan in 1987 is most timely. As in the early postwar years of 1945 and after, the United States again finds itself confronted with problems that run deep and may not be solved by ordinary measures. Incredibly, our country has tumbled deeply into the status of a debtor nation with a continuing trade deficit that could reach $700 billion by the end of 1990, in the view of some economists. A reckless tax cut in 1981 led us into a monumental budget deficit that will cast an oppressive burden on our children if we cannot bring ourselves to reduce it substantially. While the wealth of the well-to-do has soared, the plight of the poor and minorities has worsened, with grave portents for the future stability of our society. The most awesome problem of all is the senseless accumulation of mountains of nuclear warheads.

In sum, as was the case in 1947 when hopes for a constructive peace after years of global warfare were frozen in the cold war with the Soviets, these times also call for remedies that are drastic, unique, generous, and farsighted. These are descriptions that still apply to the Marshall Plan and endow the memory of it with inspiration as we seek to solve our current difficulties. It is not that our problems call for a Marshall Plan, but they do call for the kind of professionalism, daring, inventiveness, and sacrifice that were exhibited in our struggles to preserve freedom and democracy after the ravages and exhaustion of a world war.

As White House counsel to President Harry S Truman, I was in a position to witness the origins, growth, and success of the Marshall Plan. The President returned from the immediate postwar summit conference in Potsdam, in August 1945, quite optimistic about achieving permanent settlements in Europe and Asia. While no great decisions had yet been reached, he believed the conference had demonstrated that he could get along with Stalin. Month by

month, however, I watched President Truman's disillusionment grow over Stalin's recalcitrance toward Germany, Poland, the Balkans, and Iran. Deeply disturbed over a string of Soviet violations of agreements at Yalta and elsewhere, he asked me to canvass the opinions of responsible officials throughout the government and prepare a report of my findings. With the help of my assistant, George M. Elsey, this was done in the summer of 1946. My report provided such a shocking assessment of the growing dangers in our relations with the Soviet Union that Mr. Truman ordered all copies impounded. One of the opinions recorded in our interviews clearly foreshadowed the need for the Marshall Plan a year later. After noting that economic measures could prove even more effective than guns in blocking communism, the report said:

> Trade agreements, loans and technical assistance missions strengthen our ties with friendly nations. . . . The United States can do much to ensure that economic opportunities, personal freedom and social equality are made possible in countries outside the Soviet sphere by generous financial assistance.

By the time of that report in September 1946, the war had already been over for more than a year. According to expectations, economic recovery should have been moving ahead in Europe and peace treaties taking shape. Instead Europe was moving toward economic collapse, and relations with the Soviets, particularly on the question of a German peace treaty, had become intolerable. It was in the context of these circumstances that President Truman approved plans for a vast recovery program, under preparation in the State Department since Secretary of State George C. Marshall's return from an unsatisfactory foreign ministers' conference in Moscow in April 1947.

In late spring, the plan received important additional support. Forced to cancel a speaking engagement in Cleveland, Mississippi, the President asked the then Under Secretary of State Dean Acheson to substitute for him. With the President's acquiescence Acheson explained in his speech the nature of the crisis in Europe and the reasons for the United States to furnish economic assistance. Events moved rapidly after that, leading to Secretary Marshall's address at the Harvard commencement on June 5, 1947, in effect inviting the nations of Europe to join with the United States in a huge effort to achieve economic revival.

The Marshall Plan became one of the principal pillars of the policy of the United States that saved the free world. The greatest tribute to it that I have encountered was enunciated by the distinguished British historian Arnold Toynbee. He wrote that it was not the discovery of atomic energy, but the solicitude of the world's most privileged people for its less privileged as vested in Truman's Point IV and the Marshall Plan that will be remembered as the signal achievement of our age.

CLARK M. CLIFFORD

RUBBLE
AND
COLD WAR

CHAPTER ONE

RUBBLE AND COLD WAR

WHEN "CEASE–FIRE" was flashed to the combatants at the time of the German surrender in May 1945, the once productive civilization of Europe stood choking in its own ruin. Thousands of bridges that had spanned rivers and canals lay crumpled in waters that once flowed beneath them. By the thousands, too, blasted boxcars and locomotives slumped on bomb-twisted rails that ran nowhere. Above factories without roofs towered smokestacks without smoke. In cities seas of rubble—an estimated 500 million cubic yards of it in Germany—lapped against the walls of gutted buildings that were still standing, abandoned. In the heart of Cologne only the shell-pocked cathedral survived destruction. With a look of grim festivals, towns were festooned with fallen utility wires. Bedding hung from apartment buildings, the facades of which had been torn away. The blossoms of May mocked farmlands neglected or scarred by bomb craters and tank tracks. Many a once fertile field was planted only with signs warning of buried land mines.

Recalling his tour of Berlin on the eve of the Potsdam Conference that July, President Harry Truman wrote: "The remainder of our drive took us past the Tiergarten, the ruins of the Reichstag, the German Foreign Office, the Sports Palace, and dozens of other sites which had been world-famous before the war. Now they were nothing more than piles of stone and rubble. A more depressing sight than that of the ruined buildings was the long, never-ending procession of old men, women, and children wandering aimlessly along the autobahn and the country roads carrying, pushing, or pulling what was left of their belongings." Their numbers ran into the millions, trudging in all directions. Their hunger could not be seen; it had to be experienced, as happened over and over when American soldiers went to empty remnants of a meal, only to have a man or a woman who apparently had once lived a comfortable life beg to take a scrap of Spam.

The lesson of how easy it is to destroy and how hard to restore had fallen on Europe with crushing force. When it came to the matter of putting Europe back on its feet, however, the destruction that was not visible was perhaps a more difficult problem than the destruction that was. For the business structure of Europe was itself in shambles, morale shaken. For years the various national economies had been chained to war and preparations for war. Mobilization had diverted commerce, industry, and finance from their normal patterns. A number of establishments had been transformed altogether by nationalization. Years, sometimes decades, of commercial ties had vanished. Loss of capital or the war's destruction had demolished shipping companies, banks, even insurance firms. A great deal of machinery had been destroyed or become obsolete. The values of currencies were askew, barter often a necessity. Dislocation was so thorough that in the British zone of occupation in Germany even two years later prospects were for each inhabitant to get only one new suit of clothes every forty years, one shirt every ten years, one pair of socks every four years, and a pair of shoes every three years.

From Yorkshire coal in the United Kingdom to Eleusinian bauxite in Greece, the products of mines have been the foundation of industrialized Europe. Factories could not manufacture, steam turbines could not turn, locomotives could not roll, and millions of homes and offices could not be heated without coal from such rich sources as the Ruhr, the Saar, northern France, and Belgium. Yet the battles, the aerial bombings, obsolescence, and the dispersal of miners for one reason or another had riddled the production of European mining by the summer of 1945. Massive repairs would be needed to increase the output.

On Europe's farms deterioration, damage,

IN APRIL 1945 the majestic cathedral stood all but undamaged amid the ruins of the city of Cologne, Germany. As in so many European cities, railroad and highway bridges were devastated. In Germany alone, approximately 5000 bridges were destroyed during the war.

and dislocation matched the devastation of urban areas. During the fighting, farm buildings, farm houses, and machinery had been shelled and burned. Cattle caught between warring forces had been killed. When the war ended, the cities had scant stores of fuel, fertilizer, machinery, and raw materials. Hence there was nothing the farmer could obtain in exchange for his produce. Instead he kept what food grains he did grow for his family and his livestock, withdrawing most of his land from cultivation. As a result available food in the cities declined almost to starvation levels in many cases, and lack of dollars prevented Europeans from purchasing abroad.

"If we let Europe go cold and hungry," President Truman cautioned on his return from Potsdam, "we may lose some of the foundations of order on which the hoped-for worldwide peace must rest."

This admonition hardly hinted at the vastness of the task that lay ahead. The United Nations Relief and Rehabilitation Administration (UNRRA) had been established to help cope with postwar disorganization, and the United States contributed hundreds of millions of dollars to it. Furthermore, sizable appropriations were voted for the army to discharge its occupation duties in Germany, Italy, and Austria and to provide relief for people in need. In September 1945 the United States shipped 1.4 million tons of coal to Europe and planned to raise the total to 8 million by the end of the year. Shipments of meat, wheat, evaporated milk, and other food ran into hundreds of millions of pounds during the fall of 1945. But even these supplies proved inadequate. Moreover, the emergency effort was necessarily piecemeal and thus lacking in power to start pulling together the strands of the European economy. On a continent swarming with refugees after a war that had ravaged housing, problems kept outrunning solutions. Economic prostration in the West was only part of the darkening picture. In the East, events were

A PILE OF RUBBLE is all that remains of an
English house hit by a German rocket bomb in 1944.

14

changing the political balance not only of Europe
but also of the world.

Ever since the Russian revolution of 1917
feelings between Washington and Moscow had
been strained. The Soviets never forgot that
American troops were part of the Allied expedi-
tion that intervened in Russia after the First
World War in a futile effort to derail Lenin. For
their part, Americans feared and detested the
revolutionary anticapitalist, antireligious
Bolshevik regime. The United States did not
recognize the government of the Soviet Union
until 1933. Even then Stalin's tyranny at home
and pursuit of espionage and revolution abroad
continued to fan hostility in the West. It was
only after Germany invaded the Soviet Union in
1941 that old differences were papered over,
and the West sided with Stalin in the war in order
to bring down a worse menace, Hitler. As victory over Hitler neared, however, the so-called
Grand Alliance began to unravel after Stalin
interpreted the Yalta accords of February 1945
in a way that enabled him to impose his rule on
Poland and the rest of Eastern Europe.

When the war ended with the Red Army
triumphant in Berlin, the Allies had not only to
face dislocation and hunger in their own zones
of Europe but also challenges from the Soviet
Union. The whole intricate problem of restoring
Western Europe economically became inter-
twined with, on the one hand, rising conflict
with the Soviets—the cold war—and, on the
other, historical dilemmas such as the ancient
rivalry between France and Germany and the
uneasy relationship of the United Kingdom and
the Continent.

As the months passed, the European economy
wobbled and relations with the Soviet Union
worsened. Stalin's delay in withdrawing troops
from wartime stations in Iran prompted Truman
to force a showdown in the United Nations. The
Soviets pressured Turkey for a share of control
in the Black Sea Straits. Truman balked at giving

AFTER THE WAR food became so scarce that
millions of people in cities were barely subsisting.
The war uprooted throngs who were left to wander
along the roads, their homes and sources of food laid
to waste. Farmers greatly cut back production because there were no goods in the cities for which they
could trade their crops. The food shortage became
worse in 1947 as a result of the severe winter followed
by a dry summer. The plight of hungry children was
the most pitiful of all.

THE OCCUPATION ZONES
IN GERMANY

NETHERLANDS

BRITISH ZONE

POLAN

BERLIN

SOVIET ZONE

BELGIUM

LUXEMBOURG

CZECHOSLOVAKIA

FRENCH ZONE

FRANCE

AMERICAN ZONE

AUSTRIA

SWITZERLAND

IN THE PORT of Hamburg, Allied air raids in 1943 left dockside loading cranes crumpled and destroyed hundreds of ships.

IN 1947 Germany was governed jointly by the victorious powers—the United States, the Soviet Union, Great Britain, and France—each with its own zone of occupation. France had moved quickly to frustrate the original Allied goal of a de-militarized, denazified united Germany. Their experiences in World Wars I and II led the French to favor a permanently weakened Germany. As the cold war developed, a division of Germany hardened between the Soviet zone of occupation in the East and the Anglo-French-American zones in the West.

the Soviets a postwar reconstruction loan and refused to share nuclear secrets with them at a time when the Kremlin was tense over the American monopoly of the atomic bomb. For their part, the Soviets rejected the American proposal—the Baruch Plan—for international control of atomic energy. Most sensitive of all perhaps, East and West faced one another, nervously, in Germany, at the heart of Europe, each knowing that if the other were to get control of the German nation, it would dominate the Continent.

During the war the Western allies and the Soviet Union had agreed that, when defeated, a demilitarized Germany would be occupied by the victorious powers. After V-E Day, the Soviets occupied the eastern part of the country, and the United States, Great Britain, and France occupied separate zones in the western half. Practically from the outset, Truman opposed vengeful peace terms for defeated Germany, including schemes like the Morgenthau Plan to make it a pastoral state. Having seen how the Treaty of Versailles bred political and economic conditions that brought Hitler to power, Truman favored a lenient peace that might lead to a self-supporting, nonmilitaristic, democratic Germany. Otherwise, the administration feared that postwar impoverishment might either drive the Germans into the arms of the Soviets or else make German survival a burden on American taxpayers.

At the Potsdam Conference no attempt was made to write a peace treaty with Germany. That future task was assigned to the foreign ministers. It was widely assumed there would continue to be a unified Germany, whatever its boundaries. From the beginning of the occupation, however, France, fearful of a revival of German military power, impeded steps to centralize German authority and commerce. As the German economy staggered and the occupation zones became increasingly expensive to maintain, the British and American zones were merged to save money. Later the French zone joined the merger. Consequently a single Allied zone in the west faced the Soviet zone in the east, an arrangement that was to be the matrix of a permanently divided Germany, the eastern part a satellite of the Soviet Union and the western part an independent state allied with the Western powers. Another early development fore-shadowing the ultimate division of Germany was the refusal of the commanders of the Soviet zone to carry out the Potsdam provision that occupied Germany be treated as a single economic unit. Whereas the United States and Britain poured aid into their zones, the Soviets extracted reparations from theirs in the form of great quantities of raw materials and finished products.

A sign of the depth of economic and financial troubles in Western Europe was Truman's decision before departing Potsdam to send William L. Clayton, under secretary of state for economic affairs, to London to discuss Britain's severe plight. Soon after the German surrender, Truman under pressure from Congress had terminated Lend-Lease, the vehicle for providing military supplies during the war to Allied nations, including the Soviet Union. The British had received a total of about $31.4 billion, and the sudden termination came as a severe shock to them. Throughout the war they had been forced to spend abroad such huge sums of their own money that their reserves were depleted to the point of crisis. They asked Clayton for a grant or interest-free loan of $5 billion. In response, the Truman administration and Congress were surprisingly grudging. Clayton recommended a loan of $4 billion at low interest. Secretary of the Treasury Fred M. Vinson argued that such a sum was too much. Truman compromised at $3.75 billion and Congress went along, unenthusiastically, on July 13, 1946. The loan soon proved to be utterly inadequate, the more so since the British had to use much of the money to buy American goods, even as inflation was surging in the United States.

More arresting than the need for the loan to tide Britain through a balance-of-payments crisis was the specter of famine. After a 1945 fact-finding trip Samuel I. Rosenman, special counsel to the president, reported to Truman that unless Americans could send more fuel and coal, democracy faced a precarious future in Europe. "More people faced starvation and even death for want of food during the year following the war than during all the war years combined," Truman wrote later. With European agricultural production sharply below the 1938 level, more than 125 million Europeans were subsisting on fewer than two thousand calories a day, compared with thirty-three hundred calories a day for the average American. In some parts of Europe the daily ration barely provided a thousand calories a day.

On January 4, 1946, British Prime Minister Clement R. Attlee cabled Truman a warning that famine threatened Europe and Asia. The then Secretary of State James F. Byrnes urged the president to mobilize government agencies to export every available bushel of wheat. On February 6, Truman announced an emergency food program and appealed to all Americans to cooperate. He ordered a halt to the use of wheat in the direct production of liquor and beer. He raised the wheat flour extraction rate, saying that the result would be that "consumers may not be able to get exactly the kind of bread that many prefer." Also: "We will not have as large a selection of meats, cheese, evaporated milk, ice cream, margarine, and salad dressing as we may like."

Such measures, of course, fell far short. A month later, after another warning from Attlee, Truman appointed a Famine Emergency Committee, under the honorary chairmanship of former President Herbert Hoover. Hoover had won enduring fame as head of the famine-relief program in Belgium after the First World War. Truman directed the new committee to launch an "aggressive" but voluntary program to conserve food for export. Most Americans were eating too much, the president told a press conference. He observed: "We throw too much away. There is enough wasted every day in this country to feed all the starving peoples [during the crisis]." The emergency committee first asked Americans to eat 25 percent less wheat, then 50 percent less wheat and 20 percent less fat. As usual, however, the voluntary approach failed. On April 19, 1946, Truman took the practical approach of offering a bonus of thirty cents a bushel for wheat delivered by May 25 and a similar bonus for the first 1.3 million tons of corn offered before May 11. The farmers demanded more money than that. In the emergency Truman capitulated to their insistence on an inflationary twenty-five-cent rise in the ceiling price on corn and a fifteen-cent rise in the ceiling on wheat. Soon grain was flowing to the ships instead of to cattle and hogs to satisfy the craving of Americans for meat after the wartime shortages.

As European economic conditions continued in chaos in 1946, the cold war worsened. On February 9 Stalin announced a new five-year plan to increase production so as to assure his nation of sufficient production for security "against all kinds of eventualities." Because of monopoly and imperialism in the capitalist world, as he would have it, he saw no possibility of a peaceful international order. He boasted of the might of the Red Army. To American ears such was the hostile ring of his words that, for example, Associate Justice William O. Douglas of the Supreme Court commented to Secretary of the Navy James V. Forrestal that Stalin's statement was tantamount to "the declaration of World War III."

Thirteen days later a dramatic catalyst took effect in Washington. From the American embassy in Moscow came a report from the chargé d'affaires, George F. Kennan, essaying an explanation of Soviet behavior. His 5,540-word message, which became known as the "Long Telegram," characterized the Soviets' view of "capitalist encirclement" and their desire for military power and related craving for geoaphical expansion as "neurotic." The Kremlin, Kennan said, believed "no permanent modus vivendi" with the United States was possible. But, he added, Soviet power usually retreated "when strong resistance is encountered at any point."

When the fireworks had at last flickered out, what was left was a fundamental United States policy that came to be known as containment— containment of the spread of international communism. Kennan later said he meant not military but politico-economic containment. Throughout Truman's first term, from 1945 to 1949, this was uppermost in the minds of the administration, too. Most notably in the case of the Marshall Plan but also, mainly, in the Greek-Turkish aid program, the spread of Soviet communism was to be resisted by political and economic means. It was not until the second term, with the signing of the North Atlantic Treaty on April 4, 1949, and with Truman's decision to intervene against the North Korean invasion of South Korea, that the administration turned to military containment. At the same time, the policy of containment was extended beyond resisting Soviet expansionism in Europe to resisting Communist China's expansionism in Asia also.

AT DAYBREAK on January 6, 1947, snow began falling on London. By dusk it had crowned the dome of St. Paul's Cathedral. The next day the Lake District was pelted. In the storm coal deliveries were stalled and the gas supply was reduced by 25 percent. In the worst winter in memory in Western Europe, fogs and gales disrupted shipping in the English Channel.

Around Berlin coal shipments were immobilized by frozen rivers and canals. It was the second winter after the war, and Germans were reported to be despondent from the cold. Nineteen thousand of them had been treated for frostbite since December 1. Later came an announcement that forty persons in Berlin and sixty-eight in Hamburg had died of the cold. Floating ice hampered shipping on the Rhine River. Duesseldorf reduced electric power. Paris rationed gas for houses. The snow caused flooding in Italy.

Then over the weekend of January 25-26 fierce wind and heavy snow paralyzed Britain. Lorries were abandoned everywhere. Towns were isolated. In one part of Kent a hundred miles of roads were blocked by drifts. Bread had to be carried on foot to the village of Bradhurst. In London water pipes burst all over the city. Frost even choked Big Ben. The affliction—it was nothing less—continued into February. At one time in Lincolnshire only the tops of utility poles could be seen above the snowdrifts. Royal Air Force planes had to drop food for some snowbound villagers. The numbers of persons thrown out of work in England alone because of the lack of fuel and electric power ran into the hundreds of thousands. On February 10 Attlee informed the House of Commons that just in the northeast of England nearly forty thousand railroad cars loaded with coal were immovable. Under snow thousands of sheep were buried throughout the country.

The prime minister said, "We face an emergency of the utmost gravity."

An "economic Dunkirk," echoed a member from Kings Norton.

Earlier economic gains were wiped out by the weather.

In the very midst of this disaster the British government on January 20, 1947, issued a White Paper acknowledging the "extremely serious" position of the postwar economy. British debts abroad were still growing. The obvious implica-

The Press Association Ltd.

THE EXTREME WINTER of 1947 brought paralysis on top of dislocation. These British families in the Midlands grubbed for coal to warm their homes.

TWO NAPLES MOTHERS and their four children share a single crowded room.

A WOMAN in the Greek village of Stomion waits with all her household goods. The Greek civil war, between the royal government and communist-led resistance groups, broke out during World War II and continued until October 1949. The United States found itself supplying increasing assistance to the government as well as food and medical care to refugees driven from their homes in war-torn areas.

tion was that Britain would be forced to lessen its overseas commitments and reduce its armed forces. The winter's terrible paralysis had simply laid bare a far graver condition, namely, the circumstance that the economies of Britain and the rest of Western Europe had not yet been able to rise from the destruction and disruption of the war. Even before the snow it was clear that, because of the exhaustion of the war, the end of the British imperial role was at hand in India, Burma, Egypt, and Palestine. And the list was not complete.

The implications of the White Paper and the catastrophic weather were not lost on the United States. At the height of the gales Truman offered to divert to British ports American colliers at sea bound for continental ports, but Attlee declined, thankfully, observing that "the need for coal in Europe is no less pressing." The best American newspapers were quick to sense that what was happening in Europe was bound to affect United States foreign policy. Writing in the *New York Herald Tribune*, Walter Lippmann commented that the European economic crisis could "shake the world and make our position highly vulnerable and precariously isolated."

Bad as it was, not all of the trouble in Europe lay in the west. The Truman administration was highly concerned about the security of Greece and Turkey. In continuing civil strife the Greek government seemed in danger of defeat by communist-dominated guerrillas. Turkey felt itself under multiple Soviet pressures, such as the demands of the Kremlin for a share of control of the Black Sea Straits. If, by whatever means, the Soviets were to dominate Greece and Turkey, the view in Washington was that the whole Allied position in the Eastern Mediterranean would be undermined. The road to India would lie open, as new Secretary of State George C. Marshall was soon to say. Whether the Soviets could have taken over Greece and Turkey, or would have, will probably never be known. But even when all eyes were on the British crisis, secret cables were pouring into the State Department from its representatives in Eastern Europe with alarming assessments of the Greek-Turkish plight.

On February 20, for example, Ambassador Lincoln MacVeigh cabled Marshall from Athens that to regard Greek collapse "as anything but imminent would be highly unsafe." The ambassador recommended that the United States make it plain to all, including the Soviets, that American policy was "not to permit foreign encroachment, either from without or within, on the independence and integrity of Greece."

The very next day the British embassy in Washington called Marshall's office requesting an immediate appointment for delivery of "a blue piece of paper"—diplomatic parlance for an important formal message. With Marshall away, an assistant accepted from a British representative two aides-memoire.

One said, in part:

His Majesty's Government have already strained their resources to the utmost to help Greece and have granted . . . assistance up to 31st March, 1947. . . . The United States Government will readily understand that His Majesty's Government, in view of their own situation, find it impossible to grant further financial assistance to Greece.

The nub of the other was:

In their existing financial situation His Majesty's Government could not, as the United States will readily appreciate, contemplate themselves making any further credits available to Turkey.

Although American officials had reason to expect such a decision sooner or later, the notification shocked the Truman administration. Dean Acheson, then under secretary of state, sent Marshall a memorandum, saying, "This puts up the

THIS AIDE-MEMOIRE from the British government was delivered to the State Department on February 21, 1947. In two different papers, one on Greece and one on Turkey, Great Britain informed the State Department of its intention to withdraw support from those countries. The U.S. response, in the form of prompt military and economic aid to Greece and Turkey, launched the Truman Doctrine.

most major decision with which we have been faced since the war."

The British notes expressed the hope that the United States would assume the burden of supporting Greece and Turkey. Truman, Marshall, and Acheson were all in favor of doing so. The president, of course, faced the problem of obtaining appropriations from a Republican-controlled, economy-minded Congress, which was in a cranky mood about "foreign aid."

Since Marshall had to depart early in March for a foreign ministers' conference in Moscow—one that was to have a deep bearing on his attitude toward future European policy—Under Secretary Acheson took over the task of planning a Greek-Turkish aid program and drafting a message for Truman to deliver to Congress. The consequences were to be enormous. It was not just that the United States would go to the assistance of Greece and Turkey. Nor that the president's message would go down in history as the Truman Doctrine, carrying the United States deeply into a policy of containment, first in Europe and later in Asia. But the work also would set in motion the great undertaking that became known as the Marshall Plan, officially the European Recovery Program. Simply to address the problem in Greece and Turkey made it obvious that the troubles there were but a small part of the total threat to American postwar aims posed on a larger scale by such events as the faltering European economy and the collapse of the British Empire. Before departing for Moscow, Marshall told a group of congressional leaders at the White House, "It is not alarmist to say that we are faced with the first crisis of a series which might extend Soviet domination to Europe, the Middle East, and Asia."

Even as Acheson got into planning the task in Greece and Turkey his mind was drawn to the larger problem. On March 5, 1947, he wrote to Secretary of War Robert P. Patterson noting that during the discussions frequent references were made to the fact that Greece and Turkey were only "part of a much larger problem growing out of the change in Great Britain's strength and other circumstances. . . . I believe it important and urgent that study be given by our most competent officers to situations elsewhere in the world which may require analogous financial, technical, and military aid on our part." Acheson informed Patterson that he had asked the State-War-Navy Coordinating Committee (SWNCC), forerunner of the National Security Council, to tackle the problem.

The president's address to Congress, a landmark in modern American foreign policy, was delivered on March 12, 1947, a time of foreboding over the cold war. Truman did two things.

First, he proposed that with an outlay of $400 million for economic and military assistance, the United States assume Britain's support of Greece and Turkey against perceived threats of political or military conquest of one or both of those countries by the Soviet Union.

Second, the president's theme, nurtured throughout by Acheson, moved the country deliberately into a policy of containment. The crucial sentence, which, though sometimes exaggerated by critics, doubtless colored American foreign policy at least until after the disaster of the Vietnam War, read:

I believe it must be the policy of the United States to support free peoples who are resisting attempted subjugation by armed minorities or by outside pressures.

The president's appearance before Congress to advocate a critical foreign policy measure made it difficult for members to vote against it, especially in a prevailing anti-communist, anti-Soviet mood on Capitol Hill and throughout the country. Greece and Turkey were members of the United Nations and specifically requested American assistance after the British decision. The legislation passed easily, and the president

signed it on May 22, 1947. "Our aid in this instance," he said, "is evidence not only that we pledge our support to the United Nations but that we *act* to support it." The Greek-Turkish aid program went forward that summer.

TWO YEARS LATER, when they were in Washington for the signing of the North Atlantic Treaty, British Foreign Secretary Ernest Bevin and French Foreign Minister Robert Schuman heard about the larger importance of the Truman Doctrine. Acheson confided that when the president decided to take a strong stand on Greece and Turkey, it was a signal for policymakers to proceed with plans for the recovery and defense of Western Europe.

In the spring of 1947 when SWNCC began contemplating a comprehensive plan for European recovery, several basic considerations dominated thinking in Washington.

On the economic side, the conclusion was that, despite billions of American dollars, the wrong approach had been imbedded in previous measures such as army relief programs in occupied areas, the British loan, and the works of UNRRA. Such also was Europe's deflated state that the stabilization mechanisms of the International Monetary Fund were unavailing, and the loans of the International Bank for Reconstruction and Development (World Bank) were insufficient.

The best way for Europeans to enjoy the full potential of their collective economy, as Washington saw it, was to end age-old nationalistic trading practices. This would entail, among other things, lowering tariffs, facilitating currency exchange, and cooperation among the several nations to break economic bottlenecks and increase trade and commerce. The stifling economic "self-sufficiency" of the various nations must yield to mutual interdependence. The true goal should be integration of the national European economies on the American pattern.

Americans had long believed that an indispensable ingredient in their own prosperity was the free movement of commerce across state borders and along interstate rivers without tariffs or customs from coast to coast. For that reason many Americans were advocates of a United States of Europe. No one seriously supposed in the 1940s that such a political revolution was possible soon, but hope persisted that in the circumstances the Europeans might venture some distance toward integration of their national economies. Self-help in the individual nations had not succeeded in turning the engine over. A piecemeal approach was clearly not enough; Western Europe must be treated as an economic entity. Hence economic integration became a watchword as planning for a new program went forward. The United States might provide sufficient funds to fire the engine, but the Europeans must act collectively to get the vehicle moving.

Ultimately, on the economic side, stood the conviction of the planners that European economic recovery, together with a multilateral system of world trade, was essential to continuing prosperity in the United States.

As for the strategic side of the question, friendly relations with a strong, independent, prosperous Western Europe were the highest priority of American foreign policy. Before the war Western Europe had been one of the greatest industrial, technical, trading, and banking centers in the world. In 1947 it had a population totaling 270 million. Its people overwhelmingly were skilled and educated. Its natural resources were abundant. Concern lest such a vital region—Germany and Austria were considered the most vulnerable—become combined with the Soviet Union and its satellites to form a dominant, hostile bloc lay at the heart of American strategic thinking. With the Western European nations weak, exhausted, and largely demobilized, it was considered urgently important to restore a balance of power on the Continent.

It was not necessarily the existence of the Red Army that worried American leaders. Especially in France and Italy, communist parties were bold and active and were seen in the West as posing a threat of gaining control through legitimate elections and thereby extending Soviet influence. Thus economic revival was viewed in Washington as a means of constructing a barrier to help contain communism at the "iron curtain," as Sir Winston S. Churchill in 1946 had called the political and military dividing line in Europe. Furthermore, from early days West Germany loomed in the eyes of planners as a stout and essential part of such a barrier. Germany's high industrial potential would be vital not only to Germany's rehabilitation but also to the revival of the Western European economy as a whole.

SWNCC was ready with an interim report on April 21, 1947. For one thing it emphasized the importance of keeping Western Europe in friendly hands. For another, it examined the outlook for the American economy in light of Europe's prolonged slump. It noted, for example, that the United States was then exporting annually $7.5 billion more in goods and services than it was importing. While government funds were covering the difference, existing policies called for a rapid diminution of such financing in the future. But the ability of foreign purchasers to pay for American goods with gold and dollars would diminish also as their reserves further diminished. As matters stood, therefore, "the world will not be able to continue to buy United States exports at the 1946-1947 rate beyond another 12-18 months." To make matters worse, a slight recession had been forecast by the Council of Economic Advisers. Discussing a condition that was likely to make Congress think twice before rejecting a large foreign assistance program, the report said:

A substantial decline in the United States export surplus would have a depressing effect

AT A CRUCIAL MOMENT in postwar history, Secretary of State Marshall and Soviet Foreign Minister V.M. Molotov conferred in the Kremlin. Marshall travelled to Moscow in March of 1947 in a vain effort to reach an agreement with Stalin on a German peace treaty. A core problem was reparations; the two sides diverged over how much German industry should be dismantled. Without a reunification treaty, East and West Germany eventually became separate states, the East a satellite of the Soviet Union and the West allied with the democratic powers. Nothing else so dramatically illustrated Churchill's metaphor the "iron curtain." Today the reality is expressed in the Berlin Wall.

UPI/Bettmann Newsphotos

THE BREAKDOWN of the 1947 Moscow Conference on a German peace treaty galvanized work on what was to be the Marshall Plan. On his return to Washington that April, Secretary Marshall spoke to the American people.

on business activity and employment. . . . If the export decline happened to coincide with weakness in the domestic economy, [the situation involving] prices and employment might be most serious.

Meanwhile the Moscow conference of foreign ministers of the United States, Britain, France, and the Soviet Union was at an impasse not only over a peace treaty with Germany but also over the mere writing of a statement of principles on which a treaty might be drawn. On April 15, Secretary Marshall visited Stalin to appeal for a relaxation of Soviet objections. Stalin brushed the plea aside, trying to assure Marshall that further delay would be no tragedy and that things would work out well in the end. If this observation were meant to put the secretary of state at ease, it had the opposite effect. Instead he concluded that, far from wanting order restored in Germany, the Kremlin considered drift and crisis in Western Europe advantageous to Soviet interests.

Back in Washington, Marshall gave Truman a pessimistic report on the conference, heightening the president's conviction that the Western powers must move briskly to restore the economy of Europe. Marshall made a national radio broadcast on April 28 that in no way masked his own apprehension:

The recovery of Europe has been far slower than had been expected. Disintegrating forces are becoming evident. The patient is sinking while the doctors deliberate. . . . Whatever action is possible . . . must be taken without delay.

The next day he summoned George Kennan, who had recently returned from Moscow to lecture at the National War College. He instructed Kennan to form a Policy Planning Staff in the State Department and delve into the European problem at once and then gave him a typical Marshall order: "Avoid trivia."

AN AMERICAN OFFER—
A EUROPEAN RESPONSE

CHAPTER TWO

AN AMERICAN OFFER—
A EUROPEAN RESPONSE

TO MANY OF HIS PEERS George Catlett Marshall was the greatest American of his time, if not one of the greatest of all time. As the first of the five generals of the army appointed in the 1940s, Marshall, a graduate not of the United States Military Academy but of the Virginia Military Institute, was the highest-ranking American in uniform in the Second World War. Churchill called him the organizer of victory. West German Chancellor Willy Brandt later called him the organizer of the peace. President Truman said that Marshall, descendant of the family that had included Chief Justice John Marshall, was "the great one of the age." President Dwight D. Eisenhower, chosen by army chief-of-staff Marshall as supreme Allied commander in Europe, said that Marshall was the greatest American he had ever met. Georges Bidault, then French foreign minister, said, "I put General Marshall in a category all by himself." Dr. James Bryant Conant, president of Harvard University, likened him to George Washington. In 1953, America's foremost living military man won the Nobel Peace Prize for his efforts in reviving Europe.

This vast undertaking sprang from so many events and circumstances and engaged so many minds that it is impossible to cite any single originator. Certainly Acheson, Kennan, Charles F. Kindleberger, an expert on Germany, Will Clayton, the under secretary for economic affairs, and others in the State Department played leading roles in the development. No one, however, better captured the spirit of what was to be the Marshall Plan than did George Marshall himself more than a year before it was visualized. Speaking to his successors when he retired from the Pentagon on November 26, 1945, he said:

You should fully understand the special position that the United States occupies in the world, geographically, financially, militarily, and scientifically, and the implications in-

volved. The development of a sense of responsibility for world order and security, the development of a sense of the overwhelming importance of the country's acts, [its] failures to act in relation to world order and security— these, in my opinion, are great "musts" for your generation.

Truman insisted that the new program be called the Marshall Plan as an honor to the secretary of state, even though the name Truman Plan had occurred to some people around the White House. On the practical side, Truman told Clark M. Clifford, his special counsel, that with the Republicans in control of Congress and a presidential election just ahead in 1948, it would be easier to obtain legislation for a plan named for Marshall than for one named for Truman. Furthermore, few, if any, Americans ever enjoyed greater trust in Congress than Marshall did. A program bearing his name would have a head start on Capitol Hill.

To Truman, of course, must go full credit for approving the program, for getting it through Congress, and for embodying it in United States foreign policy. Truman was born and reared in Missouri, the very heartland of Midwestern isolationism in the 1930s and 1940s, and he served as a United States senator from Missouri for ten years during the height of the isolationist fervor that flared with approaching danger of war after Hitler's rise to power. Still, he supported President Franklin D. Roosevelt's internationalist policies. The long reach of Woodrow Wilson's idealism had touched Truman as a young man. He fervently espoused the cause of the League of Nations and was dismayed when the United States did not join. As president after Roosevelt's death it fell to him to present the United Nations Charter to the Senate and urge its ratification, soon to be forthcoming. As the postwar president, Truman stood in the forefront of a potent consensus favoring a dominant Amer-

ican role in the world, to include moral, economic, military, and political leadership, support of capitalist interests, and resistance to Soviet expansion. Internationalist measures such as the Marshall Plan, the North Atlantic Treaty, German revival, and the non-punitive peace treaty with Japan constitute the formidable base upon which Truman's reputation stands.

In 1947, Secretary Marshall had a standing invitation to speak at Harvard. With events moving as they were, he elected to speak at the commencement on June 5. He wrote to Dr. Conant: "If an academic costume is required, I would appreciate the University arranging this for me since I do not have my own. I am 6 ft. 1 in. tall, weigh 200 pounds, and my cap size is 7½ plus." The letter also said:

> As I wrote you on May 9th, I will not be able to make a formal address, but would be pleased to make a few remarks in appreciation of the honor and perhaps a little more.

The little more was to make a considerable difference in the world. It was not a plan, not a blueprint, but rather an expression of an idea, a modestly worded offer. The speech was drafted by Charles E. Bohlen, a State Department Soviet expert and a future United States ambassador to the Kremlin. By the time he set to work he had seen the memorandum Marshall had ordered from Kennan's Policy Planning Staff (PPS). The group did not regard communist activities "as the root of present difficulties in western Europe," according to the memorandum: "It believes that the present crisis results in large part from the disruptive effect of the war on the economic, political, and social structure of Europe and from a profound exhaustion of physical plant and of spiritual vigor." On the other hand, "communists are exploiting the European crisis and . . . ," it said, "further communist successes would create a serious danger to American security." Only three months after Truman's speech on Greek-Turkish aid the PPS recommended that the new program should remove the misconception that the Truman Doctrine "is a blank check to give economic and military aid to any area in the world where the communists show signs of being successful." As for the nature of the new plan, the PPS declared:

It would be neither fitting nor efficacious for this Government to undertake to draw up unilaterally . . . a program designed to place Europe on its feet economically. . . . The formal initiative must come from Europe; the program must be evolved in Europe; and the Europeans must bear the basic responsibility for it. . . . The role of this country should consist of friendly aid in the drafting of a European program and of the later support of such a program.

The memorandum stressed that the program must be a joint one, agreed to by the several European nations. The request for American support must come as a joint request from a group of friendly nations, not as a series of isolated and individual appeals. In sum:

The European program must envisage bringing western Europe to a point where it will be able to maintain a tolerable standard of living on a financially self-supporting basis. It must give hope of doing the whole job. This program must give reasonable assurance that if we support it, this will be the last such program we shall be asked to support in the foreseeable future.

These recommendations were embodied in Marshall's low-keyed address under the elms in the Harvard Yard.

"The truth of the matter is," he said, "that Europe's requirements for the next three or four years of foreign food and other essential products—principally from America—are so much greater than her present ability to pay that she must have substantial additional help or face

ONE of the most distinguished and powerful Americans of the postwar period, Dean G. Acheson served as under secretary of state under George Marshall and, upon Marshall's retirement, as secretary of state from 1949 to January 1953. With President Truman's trusting support, Acheson had a profound impact on American foreign policy in the cold war. He was the author of the Truman Doctrine and in the forefront of the architects of the Marshall Plan. Even before Marshall's speech at Harvard, Acheson publicly signaled the direction in which American policy was moving. In a speech on May 8, 1947, he suggested that Europe was sinking into its death throes and could be rescued only by massive American financial assistance.

DEPARTMENT OF STATE
Policy Planning Staff

May 23, 1947

Mr. Acheson:

Attached is the first recommendation of the
Planning Staff. It deals with the question of aid
to western Europe.

If approved it should serve as a general orien-
tation, both for operations and for planning in the
immediate future.

It is only a few days since the Planning Staff,
with an incomplete and provisional complement of
personnel, was able to begin to give attention to
the substance of its work. Normally, I would consider this far too short a time in which to consider
and make recommendations on matters of such importance. But I recognize that the need for a program
of action on this problem is urgent and the best
answer we can give today is perhaps more useful than
a more thoroughly considered study one or two months
hence.

If the views set forth here meet with the approval of the Secretary and yourself, we will make
this paper the basis of further planning.

George F. Kennan

THIS LETTER *from George Kennan to Dean
Acheson accompanied the Policy Planning Staff
recommendation for what would become the Marshall
Plan. In view of the urgency of the problem, the report was prepared in less than two weeks. Kennan
recognized that "the best answer we can give today is
perhaps more useful than a more thoroughly considered study one or two months hence."*

GEORGE F. KENNAN, *head of the State Department Policy Planning Staff, conferring with William
L. Clayton, Assistant Secretary of State for Economic
Affairs. Though the Marshall Plan had no single
author, Kennan and Clayton, along with Dean
Acheson, were its foremost drafters. It was named for
Marshall because of his indispensable role, his influence, and his extraordinary prestige with Congress
and the American people.*

The Stamp Act *by Marcus for the* New York Times

*M*OLOTOV'S *rejection of the Marshall Plan was seen as one more refusal on the part of the Soviets to participate in postwar stabilization efforts.*

*I*N THIS PHOTO *dated June 1947, Foreign Ministers Molotov, Bidault, and Bevin appear to be posing arm-in-arm before meeting to discuss Marshall's economic proposal. Closer examination discloses that the photo could be a montage, perhaps created to express wishful thinking.*

DELEGATIONS from France, Great Britain, and the U.S.S.R. met in Paris in late June 1947 to discuss Marshall's proposal. Molotov ended the talks after several days, stating that the Soviet government "rejects this plan as totally unsatisfactory." Molotov's walkout left Europe more divided than ever at the "iron curtain." A new phase had opened in the political conflict—the cold war—between the Soviets and the West.

economic, social, and political deterioration of a very grave character."

IN LONDON, Foreign Secretary Ernest Bevin, a stalwart of the Labor government, was listening to a radio when BBC reported from Washington on Marshall's address. The effect, he recalled, was like that of finding a lifeline dropped to him. "It seemed to bring hope where there was none," he said. "The generosity of it was beyond my belief. It expressed a mutual thing. It said, 'Try and help yourself and we will try to see what we can do. Try and do the thing collectively, and we will see what we can put into the pool.'"

Bevin headed with dispatch for Paris to take up Marshall's offer with Bidault. With his dock worker's background, one of Bevin's handicaps was his poor French pronunciation, and in all innocence he sometimes addressed the French foreign minister as Bidet.

Since, under Marshall's terms, the initiative must come from European nations as a group, Bevin and Bidault had to formalize a procedure, a problem that brought up the question of the Soviet Union. Marshall's offer had been open-ended as to the number of participants. Playing it straight in his address, he did not exclude any nation, even though numerous Washington officials worried that, if the Kremlin were invited and accepted, Congress in its prevailing mood would never vote money for Soviet aid. On the other hand, Kennan and others doubted the likelihood of any postwar settlement with Moscow.

Improbable as it might be that the Soviets would participate in the recovery program, Bevin and Bidault felt they should issue an invitation. Late in June, Soviet Foreign Minister Vyacheslav M. Molotov joined them in Paris. He hardly had time to enjoy the chestnut trees. After five days without any agreement he walked out and went home with his staff of ninety-one.

WHEN SECRETARY MARSHALL broached his plan for postwar recovery, he insisted that the Europeans must list their own requirements and draw up their own program. The task was undertaken by the sixteen-nation Committee for European Economic Cooperation, which began its work on July 12, 1947, in the Grand Dining Room of the French Foreign Office in Paris.

Furthermore, the Kremlin blocked Poland, Yugoslavia, Romania, and Czechoslovakia from joining. Stalin told the Czechs that the Marshall Plan was an attempt to form a Western bloc and isolate the Soviet Union. Molotov called it a plan to intervene in Soviet affairs. What he had wanted in Paris was for the United States to state at the outset how much assistance it was willing to grant. The Soviets' walkout deepened the rift between East and West.

To get things moving, Bevin and Bidault then issued invitations to a group consisting of sixteen nations to meet in Paris as the Committee for European Economic Cooperation (CEEC) to draw up a list of needs for American assistance. The members were Austria, Belgium, Denmark, France, Greece, Great Britain, Iceland, Ireland, Italy, Luxembourg, the Netherlands, Norway, Portugal, Sweden, Switzerland, and Turkey.

Meeting throughout the summer of 1947 under the chairmanship of the distinguished British philosopher and diplomat, Sir Oliver Franks, now Lord Franks, the CEEC was tossed by powerful cross-currents. Recommendations being urged by the United States, particularly those looking toward economic integration of Europe and creation of supranational agencies to regulate commerce, confronted the various European representatives with great difficulties. Submitting to the decisions of supranational institutions, for example, would be tantamount to peeling off a layer or two of sovereignty, an exercise that does not come naturally to nations. History does not abound with examples of voluntary surrender of sovereignty on any scale. Some views of planners in Washington, while eminently logical to them, seemed wrenching and revolutionary to planners in Europe. Indeed a signal accomplishment of the Marshall Plan was that it was able to encourage and nudge great powers to move an inch this way and an inch that and thus give impetus to historic reforms like the Schuman Plan for a European Coal and Steel Community and,

A KEY FIGURE in the formative days of the Marshall Plan was Sir Oliver Franks, later Lord Franks, a distinguished British philosopher and diplomat who also served as British Ambassador to the United States. He was the chairman of the Committee for European Economic Cooperation, which at the 1947 Paris Conference drafted the first four-year program of Europe's recovery needs.

FRENCH FOREIGN MINISTER Georges Bidault officiated at the opening of the Paris Conference. At different times in postwar France Bidault was foreign minister and premier. A Jesuit-educated historian, teacher, and editor, he had played a daring role in the French resistance during the war, a path to political power for many of his generation. As foreign minister, one of his aims was to prevent Germany from again gaining economic ascendancy over France.

ultimately, the Common Market. None felt a more compelling interest in resisting some of Washington's most cherished proposals than Britain and France.

Hard pressed though they were, the British remained at the head of the sterling bloc, then still the largest multilateral trading system in the world. Britain did not want to jeopardize that role by integrating its economy with the continental economies. What is more, it did not consider itself merely another European country. It aspired to a distinctive role, standing between the United States and continental Europe. It had no wish to yield its historic special relationship with the United States by getting tied too closely to the Continent. Moreover, the Labor government, which had come to power shortly after Germany's surrender in 1945, was busy establishing socialism in Great Britain. Labor party leaders did not care to have any overseas planners or supranational agency telling them how they should allot their resources.

In 1945 the French had entered the postwar period steeped in recollections of three invasions of their land by the Germans since 1870. With Germany now in ruins France wanted to assure its own future military security and superior economic position, vis-a-vis the Germans, through a number of steps, including detachment of the Ruhr from the rest of Germany. This idea was opposed by the Americans and the British on the grounds that Ruhr coal and steel were needed for the economic revival of Germany. The French priority was not German revival but their own—in the design of the Monnet Plan, a recovery program authored by the economist Jean Monnet. The French continually sought arrangements which, in American eyes, were, as the historian Michael J. Hogan writes, "vehicles for promoting the economic and political ambitions of the French government at the expense of German recovery." The turnabout that witnessed Franco-German cooperation and com-

By LATE FALL 1947, when Marshall left for the Council of Foreign Ministers meeting in London, President Truman was already referring to the pending European-aid legislation as the "Marshall Plan."

ity in the ensuing years is one of the salutary chapters of modern European history.

The summer-long meeting of the CEEC in Paris was a labor of endless complexities turned up from every nook and cranny of sixteen different national economies in Europe. In addition, no one on either side of the Atlantic could know in advance how Congress would react to the program or how much money it would be willing to appropriate. Thus while the drafting was supposed to be a European task, American officials inevitably became involved, causing much give-and-take over the size and nature of the plan the CEEC would present to the Truman administration. By and large, the dollar volume of the aid to be requested was based on the projected balance-of-payments deficits of the participating countries with North America—in other words, on the minimum amount each country would need for purchases in the next three or four years if it had the gold or the dollars. Washington learned with dismay that an early proposed grand total was $28 billion, a figure that would have raised the Capitol dome. By the time of the final draft in September 1947, the figure had been reduced to about $22.3 billion. Clayton came much closer to what Congress would approve, though still nearly $3 billion on the high side, when he proposed $16 billion for the years 1948-1951.

The CEEC report said that the participating countries would strive to raise agricultural production to prewar levels and achieve an even larger increase in industrial production. The would commit themselves to reducing trade barriers. Furthermore, the participants would overcome inflation and stabilize their internal finances. They would expand exports to eliminate the "dollar gap." And they would establish a continuing organization—it was called the Organization for European Economic Cooperation—to promote growing economic cooperation among its sixteen members.

Ernest Bevin, foreign secretary of Great Britain, addresses the Paris Conference. From the start Bevin's influence on the strategic currents in which the Marshall Plan sailed was powerful. Described by a contemporary as "massive, rude, and strong as a Stonehenge cromlech," he was to fight hard to preserve the independent position he cherished for Great Britain.

The shadow lengthens

THESE EDITORIAL CARTOONS, *by Marcus for the* New York Times, *illustrated the debate in Congress over the Marshall Plan legislation. Those opposed argued that the United States could not afford to foot the bill, while those in favor maintained that Soviet expansionism had to be checked. Soviet moves, notably the communist coup in Czechoslovakia in March 1948, finally squelched opposition to passage of the legislation.*

TRUMAN MOVED expeditiously to win public and congressional support. In the face of widespread concern that the United States did not have the material resources to support such a program on top of its own booming postwar economy, he had appointed a committee headed by Secretary of the Interior Julius A. Krug to study the question. On October 18 the administration made public its report, holding that the committee's inventory of American resources showed that the United States could furnish Europe with materials required without damaging national security or lowering the standard of living. The study was measured against a putative $20 billion, four-year program.

Truman also had appointed a committee of nineteen citizens from different fields, headed by Secretary of Commerce W. Averell Harriman, to inquire into the merits of the Marshall Plan. The President's Committee on Foreign Aid concluded that the United States "has a vital interest—humanitarian, economic, strategic, and political" in helping Europe recover. Their report, published on November 8, recommended that Congress appropriate between $12.7 billion and $17.2 billion for the plan for the next four years. By this time the Marshall Plan had become a generally popular bipartisan cause. When the American people came to understand the dire straits in which their European allies were caught, a surge of altruism flowed into the stream that was moving the plan forward. Civic, religious, and educational organizations were to support it for humanitarian reasons in congressional hearings and elsewhere.

Any undertaking as closely involved as it was with national security, however, had to stand or fall on its importance to national goals. Historically, the United States could not tolerate hostile, single-power domination of Europe, such as Germany under Hitler. A critical American goal following the war, therefore, was stabilization of Western Europe through revival of its economy, thus averting a vacuum into which Soviet influence and power might otherwise move. A corresponding goal, of course, was prosperity in the United States. Americans had feared that demobilization after the war could cause a reversion to deflation and unemployment such as the country had experienced in the 1930s. Although this did not happen, the signs in 1947 of a recession heightened the desire for more exports just as the economies of Europe were running dry. Consequently, the Marshall Plan had a wide appeal to businessmen, bankers, workers, and farmers, including farmers who grew cotton and tobacco. Their hopes were not in vain. The years of the Marshall Plan, when much of the money was spent in the United States for food and manufactured products, were prosperous ones for Americans.

The expectation was that the president would submit the Marshall Plan to the second session of the Eightieth Congress when it convened in January 1948, but Europe's economic crisis had grown too severe to brook that much delay. The year 1947 was a wicked one in Europe. After the bitter cold of January and February came a severe drought in August and September. Things moved in a savage circle. Because of the heat and drought of summer, the ensuing winter of 1948 loomed as another torment owing to crop failures. It was imperative that the United States provide interim assistance before the Marshall Plan could take full effect under a law yet to be passed. Truman, therefore, called a special session of Congress for November 17 to consider a request for $597 million in immediate aid, as well as legislation to deal with rising prices at home. The week prior to the session Marshall and his associates testified before a joint hearing of the Senate Foreign Relations and House Foreign Affairs committees. Marshall said that Italy would be "at the end of the tether" by December 1 and that France would run out of funds for fuel and food by December 31.

Watch your step!

IN NOVEMBER 1947, Secretary of State Marshall, accompanied by Under Secretary of State Robert Lovett, appeared before the Senate Foreign Relations Committee to defend the need for European aid.

Austria's financial resources were almost exhausted.

Truman appeared before the joint session of Congress to appeal for emergency assistance to the three countries, "if their political and economic systems are not to disintegrate." Congress approved $522 million for Austria, Italy, and France and $18 million for China to appease Republicans who were stewing over the administration's unwillingness to do more to help Generalissimo Chiang Kai-shek defeat the Chinese Communists. A month after his appeal for interim aid Truman then sent up a message on December 19 asking for the approval of the Marshall Plan, or, as it now became known officially, the European Recovery Program (ERP).

"We must decide," he said, "whether or not we will complete the job of helping the free nations of Europe to recover from the devastation of war. Our decision will determine in large part the future of the people on that continent. . . . Our deepest concern with European recovery . . . is that it is essential to the maintenance of the civilization in which the American way of life is rooted."

He set forth the rationale and functions of the ERP. It was a recovery program—not a relief program, which would have been another piecemeal attack on the problem. The recipients had agreed to act jointly "to achieve closer economic ties among themselves and to break away from self-defeating actions of narrow nationalism." They also would strive to increase production so there would be more exports to pay for necessary imports. They would set about to put their own finances in order and curb inflation. The president recapitulated the value of the ERP to the United States. The United States would suffer if world trade were stifled by a European collapse. European recovery was essential to the health of the American economy. Finally, continual demoralization of Western Europe would open the way for communist ad-

THE MAYOR of Meriden, Connecticut, asks for contributions for European relief. Cities throughout the United States organized collections of money, clothing, food, and toys. When the American people began to comprehend the dire straits in which their European allies were caught, a surge of altruism flowed into the stream that was moving the Marshall Plan forward. Civic, religious, and educational organizations were to support it for humanitarian reasons in congressional hearings and elsewhere.

vances in the West.

Truman recommended that Congress authorize a total of $17 billion for the ERP for the four years from April 1, 1948, to June 30, 1952, the projected life of the program. Under congressional procedure the annual amounts had to be debated each year, so there were many modifications along the way. Ultimately, the United States allotted to the participating countries a total of $13.3 billion, mostly in grants. To grasp the magnitude of the undertaking it is necessary to recall that in today's dollars the cost would have been slightly more than $60 billion. How Congress could have been induced to spend so much on foreign aid is explained to some extent by the fact that ERP funds were looked upon as part of the outlay for national security. One purpose of the program was to contain Soviet communism at the iron curtain. Hence Truman was able to hold the total annual defense budget to around $13 billion—a speck next to modern defense budgets—until the outbreak of the Korean War in 1950. When considered to be, in effect, part of the comparatively small national security budget, the ERP did not seem altogether exorbitant.

This is not to say there was not some staunch opposition. Congress reconvened in January 1948 only months ahead of the national party conventions and the presidential election. Conservative Republicans, their anti-New Deal fervor not yet extinguished, had returned to Washington, preaching budget-cutting. One of the leading contenders for his party's nomination was the Senate minority leader, Senator Robert A. Taft of Ohio, son of President William Howard Taft and himself the bearer of the sobriquet "Mr. Republican." An isolationist by the standards of the day and a critic of Roosevelt's public works programs in the Great Depression, he now charged that Truman was creating a global New Deal, with the United States playing the role of Santa Claus. He main-

tained that the Marshall Plan would create not only false prosperity at home but would also lead to higher taxes and economic controls. Still, Taft's attacks were directed not at killing the ERP but, unsuccessfully, at scaling it down. When the final vote came in the Senate on the Foreign Assistance Act of 1948, he was absent but recorded as paired for the bill.

Former President Hoover took a similar stand. While granting the importance of containing Soviet expansionism through economic power, he wrote to the Senate Foreign Relations Committee recommending, among other things, that the proposed $6.8 billion for the first fifteen months of the program be cut to $4 billion. The next day Truman told a press conference, "I just don't approve of Mr. Hoover's statement."

Opposition from the left was spearheaded by the denunciations from Roosevelt's former vice-president, Henry A. Wallace, who was himself to become a candidate for president on the Progressive party ticket in 1948 and all but prevent Truman's re-election. Emotionally caught up in left-wing animosity to the administration's cold-war, anti-Soviet policies, Wallace branded the Marshall Plan a cardinal example of American imperialism.

In the Senate, where the issue of congressional approval would be decided, backing for Wallace's views was totally lacking. For the views of Taft and Hoover, support was scattered among seventeen senators, Republicans overwhelmingly, from the Rocky Mountain states, the South, and the Midwest, where the isolationist opinions of the *Chicago Tribune* were still influential. What counted in the end was the bipartisan support of foreign relations that had sprung up during the war and was well tended during the Marshall Plan debate by Senator Arthur H. Vandenberg, a Michigan Republican who held the influential posts of chairman of the Foreign Relations Committee and president *pro tem* of the Senate. He was a former isolationist who had switched positions when the global war convinced him that the United States could not withdraw from the rest of the world. He, too, was an aspirant to the Republican presidential nomination in 1948. Immensely enjoying his role as a statesman, he had, offstage, an amiable, small-town, almost banal manner, not entirely unsuited to the former cigar-smoking editor of the *Grand Rapids Herald*. He once wrote short stories and composed a popular ballad to a reigning movie queen, Bebe Daniels, entitled, "Bebe, Bebe, Bebe—Be Mine." He was credited with having authored the Republicans' 1920 campaign slogan, "With Harding at the Helm, We Can Sleep Nights," and may have coined "Back To Normalcy." On the desk in his Senate office was a sign, "This, Too, Shall Pass."

During the 1948 debate and again in 1949 when the Senate considered the North Atlantic Treaty and the related Mutual Defense Assistance bill, Vandenberg was quick with the deft compromise that kept enough Republicans in line on the roll call, yet left the legislation undamaged. In one particular respect he made an important mark on the European Recovery Program. The legislation provided that the program was to be run by a new independent agency, the Economic Cooperation Administration, the administrator of which would have broad control over the operations of the whole program. Truman decided he would turn the task over to Dean Acheson, who had recently resigned as under secretary of state to return to law practice with the prestigious Washington firm of Covington & Burling. Vandenberg would not hear of such an appointment. It was not that he was hostile to Acheson but rather that he knew that the Republican majority of the Senate, which was going along with the Democratic administration on the ERP, would balk at approving the sometimes supercilious Acheson. Vandenberg and Truman had been friends when the latter was a senator,

and they worked well together in their respective current roles. Vandenberg told the president that the ECA administrator must be a Republican and must be a businessman. Congress and the administration were in agreement that the ERP should both draw upon the resources of and foster the important position of private enterprise on both sides of the Atlantic. In a curious reversal of constitutional roles the senator then "nominated" Paul G. Hoffman, president of the Studebaker Corporation, automobile manufacturers, as economic cooperation administrator, and the president confirmed him. It proved a felicitous choice.

Suddenly, at the end of February 1948, with the debate continuing, Washington was in shock. The communists staged a coup in Czechoslovakia. Ousted was a government whose origins dated to the founding of the Czech republic with the assistance of President Woodrow Wilson after the First World War. Because of that association Americans felt a sentimental attachment to Czechoslovakia and its first president, Thomas G. Masaryk. At the time of the coup dragging Czechoslovakia behind the iron curtain, his American-educated son, Jan Masaryk, a liberal, was foreign minister. Washington had scarcely digested the news of the coup when it was seared by a bulletin that Masaryk had been hurled or had jumped to his death from a building in Prague. What gravely concerned administration officials was that the coup would encourage other communist action in Western Europe, particularly in Italy, where elections were scheduled for April 18. With the debate on the recovery program nearing an end, Vandenberg declared, "Time is of the essence in doing whatever we are going to do." No chance remained now that the program would be damaged. Not Truman nor Marshall nor Acheson nor Vandenberg had in a stroke swept away all doubts about the fate of the legislation. That feat had been performed by Stalin himself.

SECRETARY MARSHALL (center) confers with
Senator Arthur H. Vandenberg (left) and Senator
Tom Connally. A Republican from Michigan,
Vandenberg was chairman of the Senate Foreign
Relations Committee. Connally, a Texas Democrat,
also a strong supporter of the plan, was the ranking
minority member of the committee.

As finally enacted, the legislation carried a significant innovation. It stipulated that when the participating governments distributed American goods to their own manufacturers, farmers, or nationalized industries, the governments make a deposit of equivalent value in their own currencies. Such deposits were called counterpart funds. They were used for reconstruction and for modernization of industry and for the strengthening of the financial systems of the respective nations and thus became an important part of the investments under the European Recovery Program.

The president signed the Foreign Assistance Act embracing the Economic Cooperation Act on April 3, 1948, saying, "Its purpose is to assist in the preservation of conditions under which free institutions can survive in the world." Thereupon things began to move rather fast.

PRESIDENT TRUMAN signs the Economic Cooperation Act, authorizing the Marshall Plan, on April 3, 1948. Surrounding him (as numbered on silhouette) are: (1) Undersecretary of State Robert Lovett, (2) Senator Arthur Vandenburg, (3) Treasury Secretary John Snyder, (4) Representative Charles Eaton, (5) Senator Tom Connally, (6) Secretary of the Interior Julius A. Krug, (7) Representative Joseph Martin, (8) Secretary of Agriculture Clinton Anderson, (9) Representative Sol Bloom, (10) Attorney General Tom Clark, and (11) Postmaster General Jesse M. Donaldson.

LAUNCHING
THE EUROPEAN
RECOVERY PROGRAM

CHAPTER THREE

LAUNCHING THE EUROPEAN RECOVERY PROGRAM

N MID-APRIL 1948 the SS *John H. Quick* sailed from Galveston, Texas, to Bordeaux, France, carrying wheat. It was the vanguard of a fleet of freighters from the United States unlike anything of its kind ever seen before in peacetime. The vessels were laden with fuel, food, feed, chemicals, fertilizers, raw materials, semi-finished products, vehicles, and equipment of one kind and another, such products constituting the bulk of ERP assistance. By June 30, the Economic Cooperation Administration had already approved grants for goods and services valued at $738 million. George Kennan was to recall, "The psychological success at the outset was so amazing that we felt that the psychological effect was four-fifths accomplished before the first supplies arrived."

As the months passed, the panorama of rebuilding was remarkable. Persons who lived in the cities saw railroad stations and office buildings being restored from bomb damage. Those who lived in the suburbs witnessed new factories and new housing for the workers going up. Country-dwellers watched new tractors plowing farms and stretches of roads being repaved. For those who lived along rivers and canals a familiar sight was the construction of new bridges, just as persons who lived near the sea could watch bustling shipyards replacing the millions of tons of ships sunk or damaged by the enemy.

Europe was fast losing its bombed-out look of 1945. Rubble disappeared. In some cases it was put to good use. In Hamburg, Germany, where at least forty-three million tons of it had been left by Allied bombing raids, the rubble was cleared by hand, fed into a crusher, mixed with cement from the United States, and poured into exceptionally strong walls.

It was the Europeans who had rolled up their sleeves and pitched in. By no means had all the work begun after Truman signed the bill. To one degree or another the restoration of Europe had started as the battle lines moved eastward. Amer-ican replacements heading from the landing craft to the front could see farmers and villagers in Normandy and Brittany patching up their houses and barns and putting hammers and saws to work on their burned-out shops, even as the Germans were falling back toward Paris. Destructive though it was, the Second World War would not have been the end of modern Europe. But by 1947-48 its balance-of-payments problem—the "dollar gap"—was critical.

The obvious and important difference made by the ERP was twofold. It changed the pace, volume, and, to some beneficial extent, the direction of European economic revival—in the process easing the balance-of-payments crisis. And it contributed to the political stabilization of Western Europe, including West Germany, in a potentially dangerous time. Giving people food and shelter and jobs and hope was an effective way of dimming the lure of communism.

The $13.3 billion that the United States provided over the life of the program was a mere fraction of the total economies of the participating countries. But ERP enthusiasts liked to say that the American grants were the "sparks that fired the engine" of the lagging European economy. Stated in more scholarly terms, Stephen A. Schuker called the assistance the "crucial margin" that made it possible for Europeans to help themselves. Writes Michael Hogan, "It facilitated essential imports, eased production bottlenecks, encouraged higher rates of capital formation, and helped to suppress inflation, all of which led to gains in productivity, improvement in trade, and an era of social peace and prosperity more durable than any other in modern European history."

Upon passage of the Foreign Assistance Act, the Economic Cooperation Administration sprang to life with the celerity of some of the wartime agencies after Pearl Harbor. If ever there was a head of a sensitive government agency who made all friends and no enemies it

FRETTING over the efforts of the Soviets to win the allegiance of Western Europeans to communism, members of Congress demanded that supplies shipped to Europe under the Marshall Plan be clearly marked so that there could be no mistaken impression as to who had supplied the assistance. These labels were placed on cartons, sacks, and machinery.

was Paul Hoffman. He had a great salesman's cheerful combination of tact and persuasiveness, underpinned by a sure sense of the purposes of the ERP. His credo was that Europe could be saved by producing, and his forte was convincing those who worked for him. He moved with the assurance of a man who believed in his product, a characteristic that had set him on the road to success in Los Angeles before the First World War. At that time the Studebaker was a popular automobile, and no one knew how to sell it better than Hoffman. He made his first million by the time he was thirty-four and went on to become president of the Studebaker Corporation. As a well-known business executive he was appointed in 1947 to the president's Committee on Foreign Aid, of which he was one of the leaders. That position prepared him for a fast start when he opened shop at the ECA, near the White House, in the spring of 1948.

The second-most important post created by the 1948 act was that of special representative to the countries participating in the ERP—the "Marshall Plan countries," Americans called them—whose headquarters was in Paris and who held the rank of ambassador. To this post Truman had appointed one of the outstanding American public servants of the mid-twentieth century, Averell Harriman, heir to a fortune produced by the Union Pacific Railroad. Before becoming secretary of commerce early in the Truman administration, he had served in two critical posts during the war, first as Lend-Lease representative in Britain and then as United States ambassador to Moscow. Despite a pleasant, even sometimes jovial disposition, he could be crotchety on the job and managed occasionally to irritate the British, who thought *him* a bit highbrow. He filled his ERP office with young Americans who took to the Marshall Plan the eager way their successors were to take to the Peace Corps. Paris was better duty than Addis Ababa, of course.

***T**HE VERY FIRST ERP SHIPMENT* transported
across the Atlantic from the United States was wheat.
The emphasis of the program quickly shifted to capital
goods for rebuilding the economy, but wheat was still
arriving in London in January 1949.

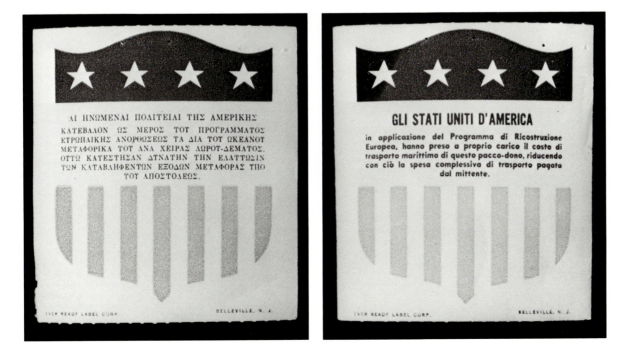

*S*O SCARCE *were raw materials that Europeans were sometimes forced to rebuild literally from ashes. In this German town, rubble from homes, schools, and factories was crushed, graded, and mixed with U.S.-supplied cement to create a strong building material.*

*P*RESIDENT HARRY S TRUMAN *confers with three of the leaders guiding the Marshall Plan, or European Recovery Program, in November 1948. To his left are George C. Marshall, Paul Hoffman, and Averell Harriman.*

As far as the United States was concerned, the ERP structure was rounded out with missions in each of the participating countries, most of them headed by prominent American businessmen. The mission staffs also included representatives of labor, who joined in the review of projects proposed by the Europeans.

The European body that corresponded to the Economic Cooperation Administration was the Organization for European Economic Cooperation (OEEC). Having evolved from the Committee for European Economic Cooperation (CEEC), originally formed to respond to Marshall's offer, the OEEC worked closely with the ECA to oversee the economic revival of Western Europe. Later it was superseded by the permanent Organization for Economic Cooperation and Development (OECD), which includes the United States, Canada, Japan, and others. Its aim is to promote continuing economic cooperation among industrial nations.

ONCE ECA GRANTS started flowing, the press was soon filled with anecdotes of all manner of bounties turning up across the face of Europe. In listing some of them in his account of the ERP, Charles L. Mee, Jr., relates how American experts showed the Dutch at the Doboelmann Soap Works in Holland how to reduce processing time from five days to two hours with a new American machine. Dispatching American experts, hundreds of them altogether, to European factories was, incidentally, an important aspect of the ERP. Mee tells how fishermen in Norway used new nets made from yarn spun in Italy out of American cotton. Imports of American leather revived the handbag industry in Offenbach, Germany, while in Denmark a machine manufactured in Philadelphia raised production at Hanson Brothers Knitting Works by ten percent. In Sardinia and Turkey, American public health officials tackled the malaria problem. In Greece, other experts en-

PIGS FOR PORCELAIN

What HAVE CUPS AND SAUCERS *to do with* SLICES OF BACON

One of our best tea-sets sold in CANADA fetches enough to buy I WEEK'S RATION OF BACON (2¼ oz) for 1,680 people

CANADA and AMERICA will buy our china—*at the right price and provided it is decorated.*
It's a good thing that they do like it as we need so much from them.
All our china decorators are kept busy working for these markets— so we have to put up with plain china at home.

THIS POSTER, displayed at shops and stands throughout Britain, tells the story of free trade in language understandable to Britons hungry for scarce bacon. Dollars offered for famous English china could pile their plates again.

lightened dairymen on why their cows licked the whitewashed stone walls: the cows suffered from a calcium deficiency.

In France, shipments of American coal kept a Lille steel factory going, and shipments of wool made it possible for one of the world's largest textile mills, in Roubaix, to stay in business. Orange juice found its way to the breakfast tables of thousands of European children, and the children of Vienna received a thousand baby chicks from youthful American 4-H Club members.

Notwithstanding, the ERP was not primarily an enterprise for delivering orange juice and baby chicks. Essentially, it was an undertaking for investment for productivity and modernization: tractors for farms, steelplate for shipbuilding, iron for locomotives, coal to turn generators, turbines for dams, electrical equipment for public utilities. Capital formation was the true story of the Marshall Plan. Richard M. Bissell, Jr., assistant ECA administrator under Hoffman, directed that European leaders should begin planning for "strategic decisions of true economic importance" to increase productivity so as to make Western Europe self-supporting. Harriman instructed chiefs of the missions in the participating countries to place "the maximum of their efforts into expansion of production." Emphasis was laid not on commodities for relief but on acquisition of capital goods. Production plans, to quote Harriman, were "the heart of the program." The first year of the ERP, writes the historian Harry Bayard Price, "was marked by a transition in emphasis from food and raw materials to tools and machinery, and from economic stabilization to economic growth." As early as six months after the start of the program industrial output improved.

American officials continued trying to imbue their European counterparts with the ideal of ending their time-worn autarky and moving to greater economic interdependence, somewhat as exists among the various states in America. It remained a cornerstone of Washington's thinking that Western Europe must constitute an economic unit without the barriers of tariffs, customs, and cumbersome currency exchange at every national boundary, or at least with lower barriers. Economic integration was still the goal of a program that stressed maximum self-help and mutual interdependence among the participating nations. After all, the ultimate aim was a permanently prosperous and secure Europe.

Always central to the task of restoring Europe was the problem of deeply wounded yet potentially powerful Germany. It was a problem of many facets: sustenance of the German people, Soviet insistence on heavy reparations that could only retard current German production, the management and use of Germany's great industries and coal deposits, German security against Soviet aggrandizement, and Franco-German relations. In American eyes one of the significant aspects of the ERP was its capacity to serve as a mechanism for integrating West Germany with the rest of Western Europe on terms acceptable to France. The first planning for German economic integration with Western Europe was done under the ERP. Secretary Marshall and others did not view German integration just as a happy adjunct to general European recovery but rather as an essential element of it. "The Americans," writes Michael Hogan, "saw economic integration as the 'salvation' of Western Europe, if only because the German problem was insoluble except in this context." After Marshall's frustration in Moscow over a peace treaty with a unified Germany, reparations having been a major stumbling block, the United States pressed for the creation of an independent West German state. Because of German resources and skills, Washington was impatient for Germany to take part in the ERP. Dramatic events portended a shift in that direction.

Even as Truman signed the Foreign Assistance

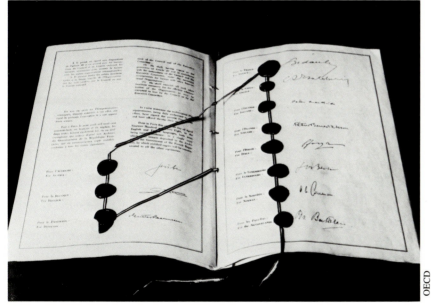

OECD

THE CHATEAU DE LA MUETTE in Paris became
the headquarters of the Organization for European
Economic Cooperation, formed by the Europeans as
an outgrowth of the original CEEC to administer and
allocate Marshall Plan aid. Today's 24-member
Organization for Economic Cooperation and Development, which remains a major force for economic
cooperation, is a direct descendant.

THE CHARTER of the Organization for European
Economic Cooperation was signed in Paris on April
16, 1948. The OEEC was the central organization of
the European countries participating in the Marshall
Plan. In 1961 it was superseded by the permanent
Organization for Economic Cooperation and Development, formed to institutionalize cooperation among
the prosperous industrial nations.

*ALMOST ALL THE NATIONS of Europe outside of
the Eastern bloc were part of the Marshall Plan from
the beginning. There were two exceptions: Spain,
which as a dictatorship under Franco was not invited
to participate; and West Germany, which did not
become a full-fledged participant until 1949. The
map shows the total amount of economic assistance—
in millions of dollars—that each nation received
between April 3, 1948, and June 30, 1952.*

Act on April 3, 1948, occupied Germany was
being shaken by conflict between the Western
powers and the Soviets. Ostensibly, the issue
was currency reform in the Anglo-American
zone, to which authorities in the Soviet zone
objected. Actually, the issue was the accumula-
tion of all the disputes, tensions, and mistrust
since the beginning of the occupation in 1945,
including Soviet opposition to the idea of a West
German government. In the aftermath of the
controversy, the joint four-power government of
Germany, which had limped along since the
Potsdam Conference, completely and finally
broke down. Thereupon, the whole situation
tumbled downhill to the decision of the Soviet
Union to blockade land and water routes from
the Western zones to Berlin, which lay deep
inside the Soviet zone and in which the Americans, British, and French had their respective
sectors. Americans viewed the alarming Soviet
move as a stratagem for driving the United States
out of Germany, if not out of Europe.

Truman made a basic decision that the United
States would retain its sector in Berlin; the problem now was how to supply it in the face of the
blockade. General Lucius D. Clay, military gov-
ernor of the American zone, proposed trying to
compel the Kremlin to back down by major re-
taliatory moves around the world, such as clos-
ing American ports and the Panama Canal to
Soviet ships. His political adviser, Ambassador
Robert Murphy, recommended direct military
action, if necessary, to reopen the highway, rail,
and water routes. Fearful that such a thrust might
trigger war with the Soviet Union, Truman ordered instead that the Western sectors of Berlin
be supplied by an airlift. It was a gamble, and it
worked. On May 12, 1949, after ten months, the
Soviets backed down.

During the thick of the Berlin crisis, which
came soon after the Soviet coup in Czechoslovakia, the United States, Britain, and France
decided to sponsor the establishment of a West

ICELAND
29.3

IRELAND
147.5

GREAT BRITAIN
3,189.8

BELGIUM-
LUXEMBOURG
559.3

FRANCE
2,713.6

PORTUGAL
51.2

SPAIN

NATIONS PARTICIPATING IN THE MARSHALL PLAN

FINLAND

SOVIET UNION

NORWAY
255.3

SWEDEN
107.3

DENMARK
273.0

NETHERLANDS
,083.5

GERMAN DEMOCRATIC REPUBLIC

POLAND

FEDERAL
REPUBLIC
OF
GERMANY
1,390.6

CZECHOSLOVAKIA

AUSTRIA
677.8

SWITZERLAND

HUNGARY

ROMANIA

ITALY
1,508.8

YUGOSLAVIA

BULGARIA

ALBANIA

TURKEY
225.1

GREECE
706.7

German government. In January 1949, Bonn announced that all West German political parties were ready to work on a constitution for a new state. On May 8, 1949, precisely four years after the surrender of Nazi Germany, the West German Parliamentary Council in Bonn approved the constitution for the Federal Republic of Germany. Germany became the seventeenth member of the OEEC and a participant in the ERP on the following October 31. The occupation of West Germany did not actually end until May 26, 1952. Until then the Federal Republic, established in 1949, had limited sovereignty, its major acts subject to the veto of high commissioners representing the United States, Britain, and France. Over the life of the ERP, West Germany was allotted a total of $1.4 billion, the fourth-largest share after the allotments to Britain, France, and Italy.

Signs of the recovery of Western Europe were clear by 1949. In some fields the economy was above where it had been before the war. Industrial output, for example, was 18 percent above the level of 1938, and agricultural production had risen. In fact, not only had the total volume of trade climbed to prewar levels, but also a number of the participating countries had progressed toward stemming inflation, balancing their budgets, and generally attaining financial stability—all important goals of the Marshall Plan. "These gains had come in part," Hogan writes, "because member states were investing approximately one-fifth of their gross national income in new capital goods." By this time, too, the ECA had extended $5 billion in assistance, enabling the Europeans to import commodities that helped them help themselves. The largest disappointment was that because of essential purchases in the United States, Europe was still saddled with an unfavorable balance of trade that left a shadow over hopes for complete recovery. The economy of Western Europe continued to improve, steadily but not to the strains of a

foto dpa

SOME HISTORIANS say the West German "economic miracle" began on June 21, 1948, with the introduction of the new Deutsche Mark (DM). Every citizen could sign up immediately for DM 40 in new notes. As the currency reform took hold, barter and the black market rapidly lost their stifling grip on trade.

Viennese waltz.

For seventeen hard-pressed, war-weary sovereign nations it was no festival to bargain and bicker over their own destinies and the flow of francs, pounds, marks, and liras, all the while being prodded by a rich ally across the ocean full of its own ideas as to what was best and well supplied with cash Europe needed. Difficult questions, such as devaluation of the pound sterling, control of the Ruhr, the pace of German revival, and integration of the European economies, caused endless and often acrimonious debate. Even the Americans did not always have sure answers, as revealed, for example, in conflicts between the Economic Cooperation Administration and the Treasury Department. The postwar turnabout was an enormous task. "A major problem of foreign policy today," Truman said in his budget message of January 9, 1950, "is the fact that key areas of the world, principally Western Europe, are faced with the necessity of making fundamental and complex adjustments to the far-reaching changes in their trade and financial relationships which resulted from the war."

And it was not as if the postwar period was one that offered respite and equilibrium in which to ponder a new order of things. On the contrary, the hard debates and hard decisions were occurring in an epoch of continuing revolutionary change and tumult. At the end of August 1949, the Soviets exploded an atomic bomb in a test, upsetting the strategic balance of power in the world. Aflame with nationalism, Asia was passing through one of the greatest revolutions in history. It was on October 1, 1949, that Mao Zedong proclaimed the People's Democratic Republic of China. The gravity of these events for the Western powers was obvious. Since shortly after Marshall's speech at Harvard in June 1947, British and French leaders particu-

WEST GERMAN CHANCELLOR Konrad Adenauer greets Dean Acheson after the signing of the Bonn Agreement granting sovereignty to his country. Negotiations during 1951 settled outstanding issues, and on May 26, 1952, the foreign ministers of the United States, France, Great Britain, and the Federal Republic of Germany signed the Bonn Agreement formally ending the occupation of West Germany.

WHILE VICE-PRESIDENT Alben W. Barkley (left) and President Truman watched, Secretary of State Dean Acheson signed the North Atlantic Treaty in Washington on April 4, 1949. A crucial provision declared that an attack on any one of the signatory countries would be considered an attack upon all. The twelve-nation pact was regarded as a shield behind which Western Europe could defend itself as it strengthened its economic base with Marshall Plan assistance.

larly were worried that a program for economic revival of Western Europe, while imperative, might not be enough. With relations with the Soviet Union in such a troubled state, the security of Western Europe might require military strength as well to provide a shield behind which a Marshall Plan could function.

After the Western foreign ministers met with Molotov again in December 1947, this time in London, and again failed to agree on a German peace treaty, Bevin took up his concerns with Marshall. The British foreign secretary suggested the need for a Western alliance to halt "further communist inroads." Marshall agreed. By stages, the concept finally emerged in April 1949 as the North Atlantic Treaty. NATO, the North Atlantic Treaty Organization, the military structure we are familiar with today, came later in a still sterner time. The treaty was simply a formal alliance, patently directed against the Soviet Union, in which the signatories declared that an attack on any one of them would be considered an attack upon all. Having watched Hitler pick off one nation at a time as it suited him, the allies resolved that Stalin and his successors would enjoy no such convenience.

The treaty reinforced the ERP objective of the integration of Western Europe. In the drafting of it American officials again urged, as they had done during the drafting of the ERP, that European nations put aside political differences and economic rivalries and cooperate on the basis of self-help and mutual aid. The ideal of integrating the functions of sovereign nations remained elusive through the years of the ERP, as it has since. Long-existing national interests tended to prevail over quick reform. Nevertheless, encouraging instances were materializing by 1950 with the creation of the European Payments Union, which replaced a complex system of bilateral trade agreements. Operating under the aegis of the Organization for European Economic Cooperation, the EPU's function was to facilitate interna-

tional monetary transactions. The mechanism, according to Michael Hogan, "broke the dike that had been holding back progress in the area of trade liberalization."

The North Atlantic Treaty and the European Recovery Program unmistakably tied together an Atlantic community with a distinctiveness not known before. In 1949 the ERP had only a couple of years more to run. But the prosperity that has come to Western Europe since the harsh postwar period and the durability of the North Atlantic Treaty despite decades of stress and disagreement have brought strength and stability to the nations that are a part of it.

"The nations represented here," said Truman at the signing of the treaty in Washington in April 1949, "are bound together by ties of long standing. We are joined by a common heritage of democracy, individual liberty, and the rule of law. These are the ties of a peaceful way of life. In this pact we are merely giving them formal recognition.

"With our common traditions we face common problems. We are, to a large degree, industrial nations, and we face the problem of mastering the forces of modern technology in the public interest.

"To meet this problem successfully, we must have a world in which we can exchange the products of our labor not only among ourselves, but with other nations. We have come together in a great cooperative economic effort to establish this kind of world. But we cannot succeed if our people are haunted by constant fear of aggression and burdened by the cost of preparing their nations individually against attack. In this pact, we hope to create a shield against aggression and the fear of aggression. . . ."

A PHOTO ESSAY

THE MARSHALL PLAN
AT WORK

A PHOTO ESSAY

THE MARSHALL PLAN
AT WORK

Also by Robert J. Donovan

The Assassins

Eisenhower: The Inside Story

My First Fifty Years in Politics,
    with Joseph W. Martin, Jr.

PT 109: John F. Kennedy in World War II

The Future of the Republican Party

Conflict and Crisis: The Presidency of
    Harry S Truman, 1945-48

Tumultuous Years: The Presidency of
    Harry S Truman, 1949-53

Nemesis: Truman and Johnson in the Coils
    of War in Asia

THE
SECOND
VICTORY

"... against hunger, poverty, desperation,
and chaos"

George C. Marshall, June 5, 1947

A PHOTO ESSAY

THE MARSHALL PLAN AT WORK

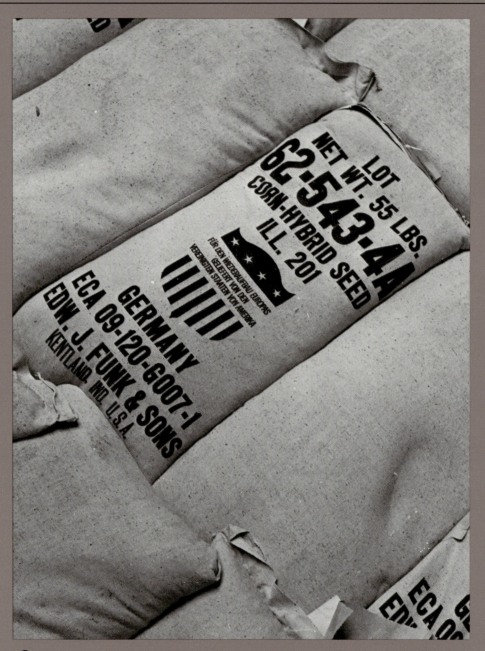

CORN SEED, *earmarked for Germany, is packed aboard a freighter in 1950.*

UNDER A SIGN reading "Berlin rebuilds with Marshall Plan help," workers construct new housing for the former German capital's homeless. In the postwar years millions of ethnic Germans, expelled from Eastern European countries, entered Germany in search of shelter. By May 1950, 27 Berlin housing projects financed by the Marshall Plan helped settle thousands of these refugees. Millions more found new homes in other parts of the Federal Republic.

IN REYKJAVIK, Iceland, a shipment of corn meal is unloaded onto the dock.

WHILE THE PRIMARY AIM of the ERP was to re-build the war-damaged European economy, the se-vere food shortage in 1947-1948 caused some of the early shipments to take the form of relief, as in the case of this powdered milk being unloaded in Greece.

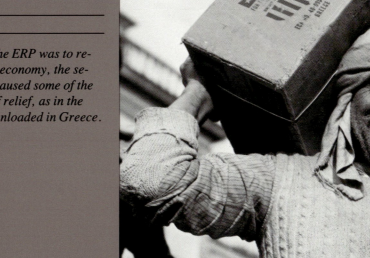

YOUNG WOMEN from the Athens Superior School of Agriculture prepare to distribute a shipment of Marshall Plan chicks, just blessed by a Greek Orthodox priest.

THE ITALIANS had a particularly difficult time restoring agricultural production to prewar levels. These women in an Italian pasta factory in 1949 are producing spaghetti from Marshall Plan wheat shipments.

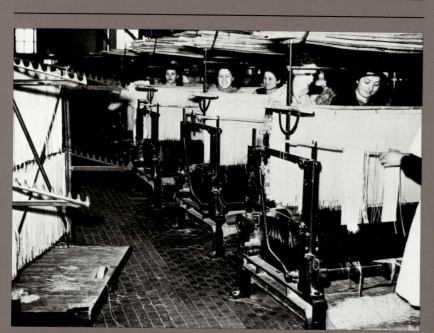

A GREEK WOMAN, at 95 a veteran of two world wars, waits patiently for her allotment of food, shipped by the ECA to provide relief.

THE ERP SHIPMENTS that touched home in the early days of the program were those providing essentials to children. Orange juice, a precious commodity in Europe at the end of the war, was welcomed by mothers.

A *FRENCH FAMILY proudly inspects its new tractor. The Marshall Plan sticker on its side leaves no doubt as to its origin.*

FATHER JEAN, a Benedictine monk, grows hybrid corn from the United States on an experimental farm in France.

WITH A $120-MILLION LOAN from the Marshall Plan, Ireland embarked on a 10-year project to reclaim four million fallow acres. These men put the finishing touches on a drainage ditch.

FOUR ITALIAN WORKERS participate in a land reclamation project made possible with Marshall Plan funds. Such projects provided sites for new houses and increased the productivity of farms.

JOINTLY WITH HIS NEIGHBORS, an Italian farmer buys a bank draft to pay the first installment on a new tractor delivered by the Marshall Plan.

THE ITALIAN FARMER and his neighbors put the tractor to good use.

A *GREEK MOTHER wears an apron fashioned from a European Recovery Program flour sack.*

*S*KILLED WORKERS *in Naples, Italy, toil to put food on their own tables and floors under families made homeless by war.*

A YOUNG GERMAN COUPLE *reads a sign explaining that these houses near Nuremberg were built with Marshall Plan funds.*

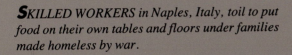

*N*EW STEEL PLANTS *were fundamental to Europe's long-range recovery. The Norwegian government built this plant, with Marshall Plan assistance, at Mo-I-Rana, just north of the Arctic Circle.*

MARSHALL PLAN counterpart funds built over 6,000 housing units for miners at Recklinghausen, Germany. The project was one of eight of its kind in the Ruhr region.

THIS HYDROELECTRIC DAM, in France, was one of many ECA-financed installations that helped offset the postwar lag in coal supplies.

IN ITALY, the handicrafts industry employed about one-twelfth of the working population. This artisan in a glass factory in Empoli displays two of the green glass jugs manufactured there for transporting and storing wine. Along with the Export-Import Bank of the United States, the ECA made loans to get this industry back on its feet.

86

AT THE END of the war, Greece's three-mile-long Corinth Canal was clogged with debris, mostly from bridges destroyed by the retreating Germans. The canal was cleared and the bridges rebuilt with $48 million in Marshall Plan grants.

TO RESTORE COMMERCE after the war, Europe had to replace thousands of ships that had been lost or damaged. Marshall Plan dollars helped provide the steel and equipment to hasten the task. These tankers, built in Belfast, Northern Ireland, were added to a growing merchant fleet.

REPAIRING and improving infrastructure—roads, bridges, rail lines—was a key goal of Marshall Plan aid. Goods stranded at factories or on farms were of little benefit to anyone. These workers are paving a road on the Greek mainland.

WORKERS inspect a shipment of rail car wheels at a Belgian rail yard.

TO GET TRUCKS rolling again between factory and market, Europe needed millions of new tires like these stacked at the Englebert Tyre Company in France. Tire manufacture was dependent on the ECA-financed import of carbon black, a reinforcing agent.

AT A HAMBURG SHIPYARD, *a worker welds a plate for one of the two new hulls being constructed.*

*T*HE MARSHALL PLAN *unclogged production bottlenecks. The engines, propellers, and instruments for this French plane factory were supplied by the ECA.*

THIS WORKER in a textile plant in Oporto, Portugal, inspects equipment purchased through the Marshall Plan.

AUTOMOBILE MANUFACTURE was no small item in the revival of Germany's economy. At the Volkswagen plant in 1952, battalions of the famous "beetles" await completion.

LINES OF RAILROAD FREIGHT CARS in Manchester, England, are being filled with sulphur brought to dock from the United States. The delivery of basic ingredients for restoration of European industry was a cardinal purpose of the Marshall Plan.

WORKERS in a West Berlin power plant chart production under a sign stating "Berlin builds with the help of the Marshall Plan." This plant, 60 percent dismantled by the Soviets at the war's end, had to be rebuilt after the power supply from East Berlin was cut off during the 1948 blockade of the city.

WORKERS haul sand the old-fashioned way at a chemical and fertilizer plant in Oberhausen, Germany, rebuilt with 10 million Deutsche Marks in counterpart funds.

IN ELEUSIS, GREECE, a bauxite mine resumes production. After being pushed through a grill by a bulldozer, the ore drops onto conveyors that carry it directly to waiting freighters.

THE SYDVARANGER IRON MINE in northern Norway, left in ruins by the retreating German army, put workers like this one back to work with the help of American conveying equipment.

A MINER *uses a pneumatic drill in a Ruhr coal vein in a mine in Essen, Germany.*

NEAR TURIN, *Italy, a welder finishes work on a 75 km oil pipeline constructed with Marshall Plan funds and equipment.*

*A*N APPRENTICE MINER *shows the mark of long hours working with coal.*

A CONSTRUCTION WORKER *in Naples, Italy, carries ERP materials on the site of a new building.*

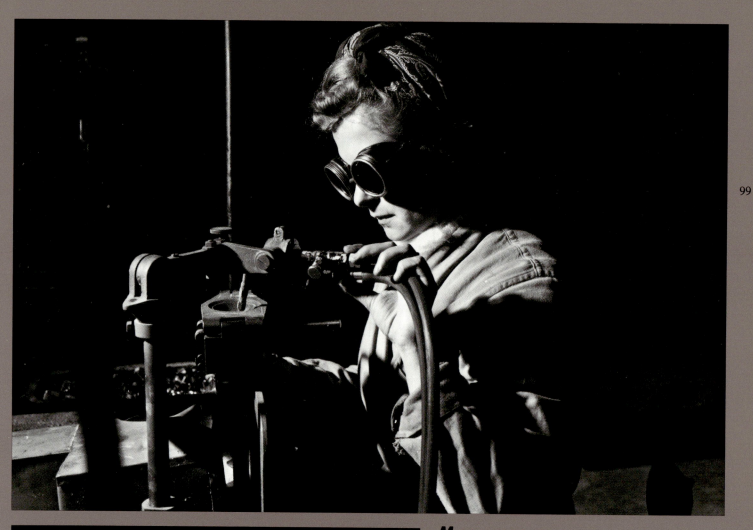

MARSHALL PLAN aid found its way to Scotland, where this worker assembles a battery for a miner's lamp in the Thomas A. Edison, Ltd., plant near Glasgow.

THE FACE of a steel worker mirrors Paul Hoffman's observation that ERP dollars "lifted people's hearts and restored their confidence."

SHOCKWAVES FROM ASIA

CHAPTER FOUR
SHOCKWAVES FROM ASIA

THE ERP HAD HIT FULL STRIDE in 1950 when it was overtaken by drastic change. On June 25, communist North Korea invaded the Republic of Korea, which was supported by the United States and recognized by the United Nations as the legitimate government of Korea. In quick stages Truman committed American land, sea, and air forces to repel the invasion. The U.N. backed him, and, in time, fifteen member nations, including Britain, France, Belgium, the Netherlands, Greece, Turkey, and Luxembourg, had military units, most of them small, in the field along with American troops. Such was the momentum of the North Korean attack that the opposing forces were almost swept off the Korean peninsula before they could stem the tide. Throughout the West the question was being asked: If the communists could rip through the South Korean and hastily committed American forces in Korea, what was to stop them from doing the same in Germany?

The outbreak of war, of course, occasioned a large build-up of American military power. But that was only part of the administration's response. Fearful that Korea might be but the first stage in the communist strategy for world domination, Congress, at Truman's request, began appropriating funds to rearm America's European allies also. This turn of affairs, with the United States moving to contain communism by military as well as economic means, had a quick impact on the ERP. The program now placed as much emphasis on military as on economic production and soon would place even more. And the shockwaves from Asia pushed matters still farther. Only five years after the defeat of Hitler, American officials began discussing the rearmament of West Germany. For at least a year the inclusion of the new West German government in the North Atlantic Treaty had been expected at some vague point in the future. For Americans, the North Korean attack ended the vague-

ness. "The most important single event affecting the future of Germany," Hans W. Gatzke, a German historian observed, "occurred not in Europe but on the other side of the globe—the invasion of South Korea." Nevertheless, German rearmament was such a sensitive subject in France that it took until the Eisenhower administration to bring it about. As Marshall had once remarked of the French attitude, "We may dispute the basis of the fears. but we cannot dispute the fact of the fears."

If German rearmament was delayed, the United States continued to press for increased military production in German factories. Across Western Europe generally the level of production was still rising. Moreover, an exciting and promising enterprise was launched by France, not part of the ERP yet stimulated by American pressures and cooperation and furthering the ideals of the Marshall Plan. The new venture was called the Schuman Plan in honor of France's ailing foreign minister, who announced it. Essentially, however, it was the creation of Jean Monnet, who had risen from cognac salesman to become the economic planner whose ideas guided French mobilization policies in the two world wars and are said to have influenced such leaders as Roosevelt, Churchill, and de Gaulle.

More than any other development the Schuman Plan, which created the European Coal and Steel Community, approached the American ideal of integration of the various national economies of Western Europe. The difficulties in the way of realizing such an ideal had been intractable from the start, and, of course, a four-year period was much too short for the accomplishment of radical change of this kind. Clinging to their own international ambitions the British resisted integrating their economy with those of the Continent. And efforts to persuade France to integrate its economy with others had constantly run up against the Franco-German problem. It had long been the American view

104

that the solution lay in bringing France and Germany together in a way that reconciled Germany's recovery with French national security. After the experiences of 1870, 1914, and 1940, however, the French were determined that in the future their economy, not Germany's, would be predominant in Europe. Thus they were stubborn about rises in the level of German production, even though the United States kept insisting that increased output in the Ruhr and other centers of German heavy industry was essential to the recovery and security of Western Europe itself.

Germany could not, however, be shunted aside. Despite French opposition, the German economy was growing. The allies were in agreement on safeguards against unlimited German remilitarization. The European Payments Union began to exert a liberalizing influence on trade. Even before the outbreak of war in Korea, concern about security was on the rise in Europe as well as in Washington. The time seemed ripe, therefore, for some change in relations between France and Germany.

On May 9, 1950, the French cabinet proposed that French and German steel and coal production be pooled under a supranational authority as a major step toward unification of Europe. Other European nations could join. In announcing the proposal, Schuman said that the European Coal and Steel Community would resolve the "age-old opposition between France and Germany." Another war between the two countries, he said, would be unthinkable and, for that matter, impossible because of the common pool of coal and steel. Monnet later had a more dramatic term: the pool would "exorcise history." According to the statement in Paris, the pool would not be a cartel because it would expand rather than restrict coal and steel production, thereby lowering prices generally and increasing standards of living. The French believed the plan would safeguard their economy and national security because through the pool France would share in

JEAN MONNET, President of European Coal and Steel Community, addresses the opening meeting of the community's governing body.

the development and direction of German industry. The high authority would be empowered to guarantee equal access to pooled resources and take steps to create a common market for coal and steel. Tariff barriers and discriminatory transportation rates would be eliminated. All of this, obviously, coincided with Marshall Plan goals, yet many differences between the French and Germans had to be resolved. The United States took an important part in the negotiations, not through Harriman but through John J. McCloy, Jr., then United States high commissioner for Germany. Truman added his weight by welcoming the Schuman Plan as "an act of constructive statesmanship." "This proposal," he told a press conference, "provides a basis for establishing an entirely new relationship between France and Germany and opens a new outlook for Europe."

The British held themselves aloof from the iron and steel community. Pravda alleged that it would be a "powerful organ of armament rings." Obviously, the plan would hasten Germany's emergence as a full-fledged member of the Western European community with an end to the occupation and greater protection against any Soviet adventures. Ultimately, Franco-German differences were resolved.

The treaty establishing the European Coal and Steel Community was signed by six members—France, Germany, Italy, Belgium, the Netherlands, and Luxembourg—on April 18, 1951. After ratifications, it went into effect on July 25, 1952. Michael Hogan later wrote that the Schuman Plan "created an economic framework that stood in lieu of a final peace settlement." The good relations between France and Germany today reinforce this observation.

WHILE OFFICIAL ATTENTION was focused on such promising innovations as the Schuman Plan and the European Payments Union, the European people day by day could

THE SCHUMAN PLAN was named for French Foreign Minister Robert Schuman.

watch the unfolding of what many Germans called "the economic miracle." They were referring to the constructive changes they could see taking shape around them and the steadily increasing availability of food, shelter, transportation, and other elementary goods and services that made their lives easier.

Six thousand modern housing units, for example, were built at Recklinghausen, Germany, for Ruhr miners. The project was one of eight of its kind in different parts of the Ruhr, financed out of counterpart funds. In just one year, ERP funds built one hundred thousand homes in Italy. All buildings in the overcrowded English slum of Landsbury were demolished and replaced by eleven self-contained communities.

The Danish nylon industry underwent prodigal growth in the early 1950s. Using modern American machinery, the Andersen nylon factory produced 8,000 pairs of nylons a day, earlier a full month's production. In Germany, refugees from the Soviet zone set up a new turret lathe factory, incorporating designs learned during a tour of American factories. With American silver nitrate Austrians made Christmas tree ornaments. Italian potters worked with clay purchased with American credits, and pasta factories were rejuvenated with American wheat for the making of spaghetti. At the other tip of Europe, steel plants were built and war-damaged iron mines restored above the Arctic Circle in Norway.

The cold war was in part a propaganda war. Fretting over the efforts of the Soviets to win the allegiance of Western Europeans to communism, members of Congress demanded that supplies to Europe under the Marshall Plan be clearly marked so that there could be no mistaken impression as to who had supplied the assistance. Farmers found such stickers on their new tractors. Workers raising new apartments on the sites of old ones labored under signs stating "Berlin builds with the help of the Marshall Plan."

Another stepping stone

AS MARCUS pointed out in his cartoon for the New York Times, *the Marshall Plan was a stepping stone toward greater economic and political integration.*

THE SCHUMAN PLAN NATIONS

NETHERLANDS

BELGIUM

LUXEMBOURG

RUHR

SAAR

WEST GERMANY

FRANCE

ITALY

THE MARSHALL PLAN indirectly nourished the 1952 Schuman Plan, a brilliant French initiative establishing the European Coal and Steel Community. French and German coal and steel industries were placed under the joint authority of an organization in which other nations also participated.

In a word, the Marshall Plan years, mid-1948 through 1951, marked a period of generally rising living standards in Europe. This was due to the efforts of the Europeans in rebuilding and to the higher productivity that the ERP helped foster. Ingenuity was endless. British engineers used helicopters to run a 1,280-foot electrical transmission line across a densely wooded valley. Four nations collaborated to build a ferry for a fifth nation, France. Dutch experts tested the models for the craft, built with Danish and English steel, and the United Staes provided two giant electrically-powered cranes. The ECA and the German Federal Ministry for Housing sponsored a competition for low-cost housing units. In the Netherlands abandoned windmills were converted into single-family dwellings.

Shops and restaurants recovered their old allure. Passenger trains were running once more. Radios were back on the market. Damaged churches and schools were repaired. With gasoline back in supply, boulevards that had been empty of civilian vehicles in the summer of 1945 were again filled with automobile traffic, increasingly sprinkled with new Volkswagen "beetles." Trucks were operating on tires that had been manufactured in plants using carbon black, a reinforcing agent, imported under the ERP. A parable of the Marshall Plan was written on stickers displayed on the windshields of cars just off the production line. Some stickers read HOME, others EXPORT. They echoed twin aims of the recovery program: greater production and more trade. Without exports the European countries could not have solved the severe balance-of-payments problems left by the war. Finally, hotels again were crowded in the tourist season.

The period 1948-1951 was still a troubled time in the world, but in Europe, at least, many of the hardest legacies of the Second World War were fading.

BOTH CONGRESS AND THE OEEC saw a strong production effort as indispensable in restoring a healthy European economy. Six months into the Marshall Plan, the OEEC nations set themselves the target, for 1952, of increasing industrial production 30 percent above prewar levels. The agricultural target was a 15 percent increase. The industrial goal was surpassed a full year early, and the agricultural goal was nearly achieved by then. Western Europe's combined Gross National Product rose from $119.6 billion in 1947 to almost $159 billion in 1951—an overall increase of 32.5 percent. Most European national economies had reached a point of self-sustaining growth when the ERP ended.

INDUSTRIAL PRODUCTION IN WESTERN EUROPE

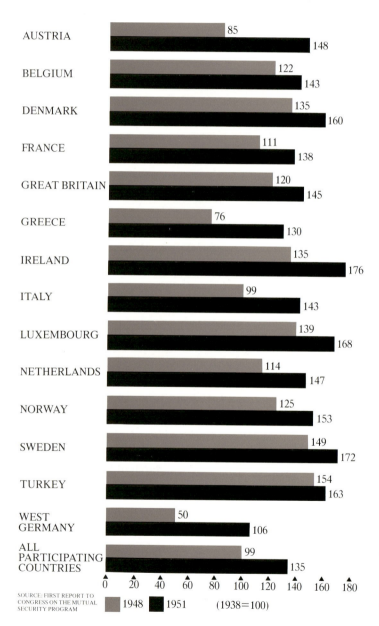

Country	1948	1951
AUSTRIA	85	148
BELGIUM	122	143
DENMARK	135	160
FRANCE	111	138
GREAT BRITAIN	120	145
GREECE	76	130
IRELAND	135	176
ITALY	99	143
LUXEMBOURG	139	168
NETHERLANDS	114	147
NORWAY	125	153
SWEDEN	149	172
TURKEY	154	163
WEST GERMANY	50	106
ALL PARTICIPATING COUNTRIES	99	135

SOURCE: FIRST REPORT TO CONGRESS ON THE MUTUAL SECURITY PROGRAM   ■ 1948 ■ 1951   (1938=100)

TOTAL AGRICULTURAL OUTPUT FOR HUMAN CONSUMPTION IN OEEC COUNTRIES

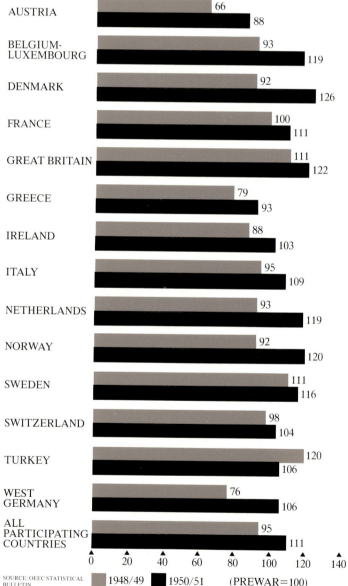

Country	1948/49	1950/51
AUSTRIA	66	88
BELGIUM-LUXEMBOURG	93	119
DENMARK	92	126
FRANCE	100	111
GREAT BRITAIN	111	122
GREECE	79	93
IRELAND	88	103
ITALY	95	109
NETHERLANDS	93	119
NORWAY	92	120
SWEDEN	111	116
SWITZERLAND	98	104
TURKEY	120	106
WEST GERMANY	76	106
ALL PARTICIPATING COUNTRIES	95	111

SOURCE: OEEC STATISTICAL BULLETIN   ■ 1948/49 ■ 1950/51   (PREWAR=100)

THE RISE
OF NATO

THE RISE OF NATO

THE FINAL STAGE of the Marshall Plan was summed up graphically by Charles Kindleberger, former chief of the division of German and Austrian affairs in the State Department. The Marshall Plan did not end, he observed, but was swallowed up by the activities of the burgeoning North Atlantic Treaty Organization. The sudden NATO expansion had its origins in Washington's alarm over the ominous world situation in 1949, particularly the news of the first Soviet nuclear bomb test. Then a frightening turn of events in Korea in November 1950 brought about a major enlargement of NATO, leading to an earlier termination of the Marshall Plan than had been anticipated.

When the Senate had approved the North Atlantic Treaty in April 1949, it did so in the knowledge that Truman would soon submit a companion program to provide funds for rearming allies—as it was said, to put steel in the treaty. For months Congress fought over this new legislation in the most intense debate of its kind since the Lend-Lease act of 1941. In October the debate collapsed when the Soviet Union exploded the bomb. "Russia has shown her teeth," cried Senator Tom Connally of Texas, who had replaced Vandenberg as chairman of the Foreign Relations Committee after the Democratic victory in 1948. Congress gave Truman substantially what he had asked for the first year of the Mutual Defense Assistance Program, with $1 billion going to countries that had signed the treaty.

Then late in November 1950, five months after the Korean War began, the United States was plunged into potentially one of the most dangerous military crises in its history, one that could have led to a nuclear conflict. Just when it appeared that General of the Army Douglas A. MacArthur's United Nations forces were in reach of final victory, three hundred thousand Communist Chinese troops sprang into battle and hurled him back. China intervened in the Korean War to prevent MacArthur from moving to the Chinese border along the Yalu River. Actually, he was advancing toward the river not to menace China but to defeat North Korea. While MacArthur and his successor, General Matthew B. Ridgway, eventually contained the Chinese attack, preventing a complete rout of U.N. troops, the war was left in permanent stalemate. The United States was also left in a state of national emergency, proclaimed by Truman on December 16, 1950. In the circumstances a stronger defense of Europe seemed imperative to him.

The United States still had two divisions on occupation duty in Europe. Despite bitter efforts by conservatives to prohibit him from doing so without specific approval of Congress, the president early in 1951 committed four more divisions to Europe. What with navy, air force, and service personnel, the four new divisions brought to more than one hundred and eighty thousand the United States military establishment in Europe. For the United States this was unprecedented in peacetime. It reassured old allies, however, that Asian problems were not cancelling American interests in Europe.

Two years earlier the North Atlantic Treaty had been simply a binding document. Now, in 1951, it was a military system with its own headquarters, staff, troops, communications, weapons, and a newly appointed supreme commander, General of the Army Dwight D. Eisenhower. Five and a half years after Eisenhower had led allied forces into a joint victory with the Soviets over Hitler, Truman recalled him to active duty in the new post. The situation in Europe became very different from what it had been when the stalwarts of the Economic Cooperation Administration had descended upon it in the summer of 1948 to try to help put a staggering civilization back on its feet. Now American dollars were being funneled

As THE EUROPEAN RECOVERY PROGRAM gave way to the Mutual Defense Assistance Program, the familiar Marshall Plan labels bore a new message: "From USA for Mutual Defense."

into Europe not only by the European Recovery Program but also by the Mutual Defense Assistance Program (MDAP). The purposes of the two programs were different, but the difference began narrowing when the ERP gave priority to military production.

The Korean War had forced a shift in "foreign aid" from economic to military. Shortly after the North Korean attack, Congress, faced with a huge rise in military spending, cut $208 million from the ERP budget and increased funds for the MDAP by $4 billion. Always eager to get in the thick of the action, Harriman left his Paris post after the Korean War began and went to the White House as a trouble-shooter for Truman. He was succeeded as ambassador-at-large to the countries in the Marshall Plan by his assistant, Milton Katz. Three months later, the program winding down, Hoffman resigned as ECA administrator and was succeeded by his deputy, William C. Foster. Instead of running into 1952, as had been planned, the European Recovery Program officially ended on December 31, 1951, with the Korean War still raging.

Nevertheless, the final eighteen months were an eventful, even a swirling and turbulent time because of the Korean War and its advantages and disadvantages for the ERP countries. On the one hand, American military assistance through both the ERP and the MDAP sent European industrial production up to a point 39 percent higher than the prewar level. Moreover, as Michael Hogan notes, war production in the United States stimulated purchases of strategic materials from overseas territories of the ERP countries. In the case of Britain, for example, this trade swelled gold and dollar reserves sufficiently that Britain required no further aid under the Marshall Plan after 1950. On the other hand, Europe as well as America suffered from a spurt of wartime inflation. Although Europe experienced nothing like the political storms that wracked the United States after the Chinese

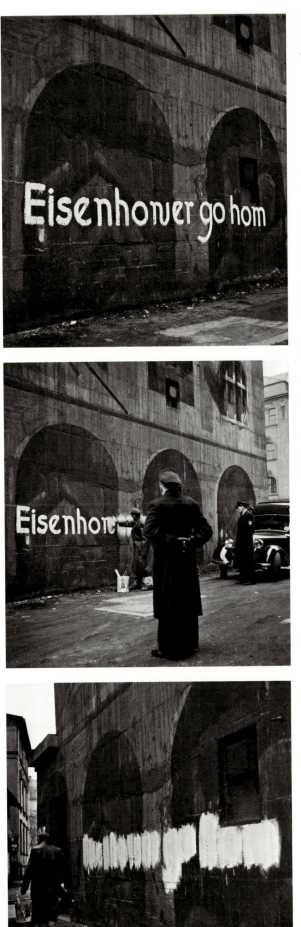

intervention and Truman's dismissal of MacArthur, the Korean War years were not easy for the Europeans. In particular, they were fearful that Korea might yet touch off a world war. Indeed in December 1950 Prime Minister Attlee rushed to Washington to satisfy himself that Truman did not intend to use the atomic bomb against China, unless things took a much worse turn than was likely. The Europeans were bitter that the United States had gotten itself into such a predicament in Asia. At the same time they were adjusting to their own rearmament and all the economic and political problems the plans posed, including the obviously approaching rearmament of Germany.

Through it all, American officials urged greater production and integration in Western Europe. Where once they had pressed for economic integration, they now also emphasized the importance of military integration within NATO. Certainly, the alliance, with Eisenhower again in command of forces, was pulling Western Europe together in a new cohesiveness that could not have been visualized when Marshall spoke at Harvard.

With less money now for new grants, Economic Cooperation Administration officials released counterpart funds for modernizing industrial facilities. Also they put to good use the relatively low-cost technical assistance program in the ERP. As Michael Hogan writes, "Technical assistance was one of the last areas where the ECA could pursue its own initiative. By mid-1951, it had expended nearly $30 million on the technical assistance program, with most of this amount allocated after the outbreak of the Korean War and nearly $8 million in the period between March and July 1951." The activities covered a wide spectrum. Capital goods industries, for example, were vital to the success of European rearmament. Hence British, French, Italian, and Danish "productivity teams" were sent to the United States to study American

*U*NDER THE ECA technical assistance program, teams of managers and workers traveled to the United States to learn American manufacturing techniques.

*E*UROPEAN REARMAMENT made progress after emphasis on civilian production under the ERP shifted to military production during the Korean War. In NATO maneuvers testing allied strength in the Mediterranean, Greek and Turkish troops greet each other as they link up in Greece.

THE RECOVERY of Hamburg, Germany, attests to the progress made under the Marshall Plan. Allied air raids in 1943 left ruined facades along Moenckebergstrasse. By 1950 trolleys carry commuters to the restored business district.

methods of smelting and refining non-ferrous metals, machine tool production, foundry practices, and railway equipment manufacturing. A German productivity team visited the United States to observe coal mining. (Those were the days before the tables were turned, when foreigners still came to the United States to learn how best to run an industry.) In all, according to Hogan, 145 European productivity teams visited the United States between March and July of 1951. They consisted of more than one thousand labor, management, and agricultural experts. In cooperation with the National Management Council the ECA dispatched 372 American experts of one kind and another to Europe to speak at management seminars on subjects like engineering, marketing, research techniques, and standardization. The ECA also supported the work of the Anglo-American Council on Productivity. The council sponsored visits to the United States of sixty-six British productivity teams. As an interesting sidelight, when Paul Hoffman resigned as ECA administrator, he was named president of the Ford Foundation and exerted his influence to have the foundation support State Department programs directed at "increasing the ability of people to produce."

A DIFFICULTY IN ASSESSING the Marshall Plan forty years later is the familiar dilemma as to what would have happened if the United States had not stepped into the postwar economic crisis as it did. On the one hand, it might be ventured that Western Europe would have pulled itself together with its own efforts and resources. On the other hand stands the theory expressed by Harry Bayard Price, the official historian of the ERP, that the program probably prevented a collapse of Europe and the Mediterranean area, with a resulting spread of communism to the west. Another unanswerable question is whether the Marshall Plan might have accomplished more if the Korean War had

not diverted some efforts to military production.

When the dilemma and the theories are set aside, what does remain is a history of progress so unmistakable as to establish a claim of high achievement for the European Recovery Program. It is hard to recall all that was done under the initiative broached by George Marshall on June 5, 1947, without concluding that it left Europe and the United States better off and more secure than they would have been otherwise. In overcoming the ravages of war the allies perpetuated in the form of a tangible Atlantic community the cooperation that had produced victory in 1945. The second victory, the one wrung from the struggle for Europe's economic revival, was a necessary complement to the first.

This is not to say that by the end of 1951 the Marshall Plan had solved the economic problems confronting Europe or had even drastically changed the nature of the European economy. Yet by most signs people were living better than they had in 1947. Morale was much improved. A great deal of war damage had been repaired. The strengthening of political and fiscal stability had been striking. As the program had moved along over the years it resulted in very favorable trends in industrial production, imports and exports, intra-European trade, and residential and commercial construction. Many of the abnormalities caused by the war had been rectified. In his Harvard address Marshall had said, "The modern system of the division of labor upon which the exchange of products is based is breaking down." If that assessment was correct, the danger was averted.

Disappointments also had to be taken into account. By the end of 1951 earlier gains in monetary stability had been eroded by defense production, and the Korean War had brought new inflation. Agricultural output had improved but not enough to eliminate the need for large imports of food. This was an important factor in the discouraging persistence of trade imbalance.

IN HAMBURG, the walls of new apartment buildings were raised from the ruins of the old.

In retrospect it seems that the Americans were unrealistic in supposing that Europe's balance-of-trade problem could be corrected in four years.

If the European economy had not reached the viable state that American planners had called for by the end of 1951, it had achieved a telling momentum. By taking a longer perspective it may be seen that the Marshall Plan was not an end in itself but one stage leading to the next stage and the stage after that one. To quote the economic historian Imanuel Wexler, "If one is permitted to project beyond 1952 and to measure the economic distance traveled by Western Europe in less than ten years after the aid program had ended, then one can, indeed, hail the Marshall Plan as one of the great economic success stories of modern time." By 1960, according to Professor Wexler, "Western Europe had become the second most important industrial and trading center in the world."

American assistance to Europe did not end with the Marshall Plan. Money for rearmament continued to flow, keeping European factories busy, through the Mutual Security Agency, created in 1951. The historian Theodore A. Wilson noted in 1977: "In an important sense . . . the Marshall Plan has remained in operation to the present day. ECA became the MSA; the MSA became the Foreign Operations Administration (FOA) in 1953; FOA was rechristened the International Cooperation Administration (ICA) in 1955; and in 1961, ICA begat the Agency for International Development (AID). Economic aid, begun on a large scale with the Marshall Plan, became a vital element in American diplomacy."

The dream of formal economic integration of Western Europe under the Marshall Plan was not realized. Except for the European Coal and Steel Community, a French initiative encouraged by the United States, no supranatural agency blossomed to regulate intra-European trade. Yet,

as Professor Hogan writes, "If viewed against the pattern of bilateralism that existed in 1947, or from the perspective of the Treaty of Rome concluded a decade later, it seems clear that American recovery policy helped to set the Europeans on a road that led from the economic autarky of the 1930s to the Common Market of the 1960s."*

*On March 25, 1957, two Treaties of Rome were signed. One established the Common Market, the other the European Atomic Energy Community.

THE LEGACY

CHAPTER SIX
THE LEGACY

TODAY'S GENERATION has largely forgotten the details of the European Recovery Program. Yet the very term "Marshall Plan" endures as a synonym for something large, bold, expert, high-minded—an enterprise that *worked*, that effectively dealt with international problems without recourse to war. Two of the new generation's able writers, Walter Isaacson and Evan Thomas, describe the Marshall Plan in their recent book *The Wise Men* as "power used to its best end."

Notable from the perspective of recent years has been the sense of the Marshall Plan as the work of sure-footed men who knew what they wanted and how to go about accomplishing it. In this respect it is pertinent to recall that the enormous challenges of the Second World War and the treacherous postwar years brought to high posts in the government in the 1940s and 1950s a company of extraordinary figures. Among those of them who became involved in the European Recovery Program in one way or another were Marshall and Eisenhower from the army, Acheson from the law, Robert Lovett, Paul H. Nitze, and John McCloy from Wall Street, George Kennan and Charles Bohlen from the career diplomatic service, and Harriman and Hoffman from business. Men of their character attracted able assistants and staffs and demanded the highest performance from them. Finally, no one connected with the task ever had to doubt where President Truman stood or to fear that his support would waver under partisan attack. All in all, it was a spirited undertaking.

The Marshall Plan was a good example of a government concentrating on fundamentals and not being driven off on tangents by ideology and obsessions. The cold war was a tragedy, and the United States bore its share of the blame for it. No doubt East-West relations worsened because the two sides went in different directions over the Marshall Plan. But the schism was permanent then. Two official American statements at the time stand out as basic. One was the Policy Planning Staff report which Marshall had requested from Kennan in 1947. It said, as will be recalled, that it was not communist mischief but the exhaustions of the war that were causing the economic and social crisis in Europe. The other statement was Truman's message to Congress on December 19, 1947, in which he said that reviving Western Europe was essential because the American way of life was rooted in European civilization. Dealing wisely and successfully with what was fundamental markedly enhanced America's leadership in the world at that time.

Nothing has been more flattering to the lasting good reputation of the European Recovery Program than the seemingly endless calls heard regularly in the United States and abroad for a new "Marshall Plan" to solve this or that menacing crisis in the world. Over the last decade or so newspapers and television news programs have carried stories reporting on pleas from leaders for a Marshall Plan for Africa, the Philippines, Indochina, Central America, the Middle East, and other troubled places. The Marshall Plan, however, may have been unique, and its like may not be seen again. Essentially it was designed to prime the pump of the economy of a major industrial civilization. No such pump exists in many Third World nations. The Marshall Plan was the product of a rare combination of elements: the enormous wealth of postwar America, the productive skills and natural resources of Europe, the similarity of laws, government, institutions, and culture of Western Europe and the United States, and the genius of postwar leadership on both sides of the Atlantic. The Marshall Plan was a program superbly suited to a particular moment of history.

THE MARSHALL PLAN was a success in terms of its own fulfilled objectives: revival of European production, a higher standard of living, progress toward industrial reorganization and economic integration, restoration of multilateral trade, political stabilization, integration of West Germany into the European community, containment of communism, and, lastly, peace.

NOTES

THIS BOOK draws extensively on such official sources as the volumes *Foreign Relations of the United States* (hereafter *FRUS*) and *Public Papers of the Presidents of the United States: Harry S. Truman (PPP)*. The former, published by the Department of State, contain diplomatic correspondence, cables, memorandums, reports of conversations, National Security Council papers, and the like. The latter, compiled under the direction of the National Archives and Records Administration, Office of the Federal Register, contain, year by year, presidential messages, speeches, certain correspondence, press conference transcripts, and selective statements. Both works are issued by the U.S. Government Printing Office.

Copious research exists in histories, biographies, and memoirs. An outstanding scholar on the subject, Michael J. Hogan, graciously made available to me a copy of the manuscript of his forthcoming book *The Marshall Plan: America, Britain, and the Reconstruction of Western Europe, 1947-1952*, which is being published this year by Cambridge University Press. Since page proofs were not yet available, references herein cannot cite book page numbers. Forrest C. Pogue also made available the galley proofs of his forthcoming *George C. Marshall: Statesman*. Published in the interim by Viking, it is the last of four volumes in Pogue's commanding work on Marshall. Other books that have been of particular value to me have been Imanuel Wexler's *The Marshall Plan Revisited: The European Recovery Program in Economic Perspective; The Marshall Plan: The Launching of the Pax Americana* by Charles L. Mee, Jr.; Harry Bayard Price's *The Marshall Plan and Its Meaning;* Theodore A. Wilson's *The Marshall Plan 1947-1951;* and *The Marshall Plan: A Retrospective,* edited by Stanley Hoffmann and Charles Maier. Professor Maier was a member of a scholarly committee that advised the German Marshall Fund on its Marshall Plan exhibit, out of which this book grew. Among others, he and Ronald Steel were helpful with specific criticisms of this work in draft.

CHAPTER 1.
RUBBLE AND COLD WAR
Truman's description of Berlin is in the first volume of his memoirs, *Year of Decisions*, p. 341. The account of the scarcity of clothing is from Hans Otto Wesemann, "The Miracle of German Recovery" in the *Atlantic Monthly*, March 1957, p. 179. For Truman's warning on hunger see *PPP* 1945, p. 211. On the question of the Soviet withdrawal of German resources see Richard W. Leopold, *The Growth of American Foreign Policy*, p. 638. Truman's quotation on the danger of starvation is in *Year of Decisions*, p. 467. His statement on emergency food relief is in *PPP* 1946, p. 106 ff. Excerpts from the "Long Telegram" are in George F. Kennan, *Memoirs, 1925-1950*, p. 547 ff. The passages dealing with conditions in England and the Continent in the winter of 1947 draw on *The Times* of London for that period. The diplomatic references concerning Greece and Turkey are in *FRUS*, vol. 5, 1947, as is Dean Acheson's memorandum to George C. Marshall. Truman's address to Congress on Greek-Turkish aid is in *PPP* 1947, p. 176 ff. Acheson's comment to Ernest Bevin and Robert Schuman is reported in *FRUS* 1949, vol. 3, pp. 173-75. For the SWNCC report see *FRUS* 1947, vol. 3, p. 209, and for the Council of Economic Advisors' forecast see *ibid.*, p. 204 ff. "Avoid trivia" is quoted from Kennan's *Memoirs*, pp. 325-26.

CHAPTER 2.
AN AMERICAN OFFER—A EUROPEAN RESPONSE
Marshall's speech to his successors is quoted in Forrest C. Pogue, *George C. Marshall: Statesman*, p. 168. Quotes from Marshall's letter to James Bryant Conant are from a copy in the Marshall Library in Lexington, Virginia. The Policy Planning Staff report is in *FRUS* 1947, vol. 3, p. 223 ff. Marshall's speech at Harvard is reprinted in numberless journals and books, including *The Marshall Plan: A Retrospective*, p. 95 ff. Bevin's reaction is reported in Mee's *The Marshall Plan*, p. 107 ff. Truman's message to Congress on the Marshall Plan is in *FRUS* 1947, p. 515 ff.

CHAPTER 3.
LAUNCHING THE EUROPEAN RECOVERY PROGRAM
Kennan's quotation on the psychological effect of Marshall Plan shipments is in Mee, p. 246. Stephen A. Schuker is quoted in the Michael Hogan manuscript, also the source of the Bissell and Harriman quotations on production. The Price quotations are from *The Marshall Plan and Its Meaning*, p. 94. Truman's speech at the signing of the North Atlantic Treaty is in *PPP* 1949, p. 196 ff.

CHAPTER 4.
SHOCKWAVES FROM ASIA
The quotation on the future of Germany is from Hans W. Gatzke, *Germany and the United States: A Special Relationship?*, p. 182. Marshall's quotes on the French attitude are from Pogue, p. 253.

CHAPTER 5.
THE RISE OF NATO
Kindleberger is quoted in Wexler, p. 249. The Wexler quotes are from his *The Marshall Plan Revisited*, pp. 252-55. The quotes from Wilson are from his *The Marshall Plan 1947-1951*, pp. 46-47.

CHAPTER 6.
THE LEGACY
The quotation from Walter Isaacson and Evan Thomas is from their *The Wise Men*, p. 408.

PHOTO CREDITS

INDEX

The sources for photographs in this book appear below. When more than one photo appears on a page, credits are listed from left to right and top to bottom. National Archives Still Pictures Branch references are preceded by NARA.

Photo research by Shirley Green.

12, 13–NARA 111-SC-206174. 14–NARA 286-MP-MISC-738. 15–NARA 286-MP-UK-56. 17–NARA 286-MP-GER-940. 20, 21–The Press Association Limited (London), NARA 286-MP-ITA-647. 22–NARA 286-MP-GREE-519. 23–National Archives Diplomatic Branch 868.00/2-2147. 25–UPI/Bettmann Newsphotos. 27–NARA CN-10113. 28–UPI/Bettmann Newsphotos. 32,33–Agency for International Development. 34–NARA 306-PS-52-2155. 35–National Archives Diplomatic Branch 840.50 Recovery/5.2347, NARA 306-NT-266M-1. 36,37–Library of Congress, NARA 306-NT-1391-6, NARA 306-NT-1391-5. 38,39–NARA 306-NT-1402A-1. 40–Lord Oliver Franks, NARA 306-NT-1402A-3. 41–NARA 306-NT-320A-31, NARA 306-NT-1402A-4. 42–Library of Congress. 43–Library of Congress. 44, 45–Agency for International Development. 46–NARA 306-PS-52-413. 49–Agency for International Development. 50, 51–Truman Library. 56–U.S. Information Agency, Truman Library. 57–NARA 286-MP-UK-67. 58–NARA 286-MP-GER-950, NARA 306-FS-211-26. 59–NARA 286-MP-UK-465. 61–NARA 306-NT-1075-20, Organization for Economic Cooperation and Development. 64, 65–NARA 286-MP-GER-1924. 66–Deutsche Presse-Agentur GmbH. 67–NARA 306-PS-52-7244, NARA 306-NT-228-5. 71–NARA 306-PS-50-3809. 72–Agency for International Development. 73–U.S. Information Agency. 74–NARA 286-MP-GREE-517, NARA 286-MP-GREE-2103. 75–NARA 286-MP-ITA-237, NARA 286-MP-GREE-184, NARA 286-MP-UK-306. 76, 77–NARA 306-PS-50-10238. 78–NARA 306-PS-51-1150, NARA 286-MP-IRE-4. 79–NARA 286-MP-ITA-728B, NARA 286-MP-ITA-298, NARA 286-MP-ITA-302. 80–NARA 306-PS-52-2024. 81–NARA 286-MP-GREE-1884. 82–NARA 286-MP-GER-1833, NARA 286-MP-ITA-676, U.S. Information Agency. 83–NARA 286-MP-GER-1979, Agency for International Development. 84, 85–NARA 286-MP-ITA-751. 86–NARA 286-MP-GREE-62, NARA 286-MP-UK-18. 87–NARA 286-MP-GREE-205, NARA 286-MP-BELG-87, U.S. Information Agency. 88–U.S. Information Agency. 89–NARA 286-MP-GER-858. 90, 91–U.S. Information Agency. 92–U.S. Information Agency, NARA 286-MP-GER-1230. 93–NARA 286-MP-UK-221E, NARA 286-MP-GER-1721, NARA 286-MP-GER-1743. 94–NARA 286-MP-GREE-1942, NARA 286-MP-NOR-102 bis. 95–NARA 286-MP-GER-2030, U.S. Information Agency. 96–NARA 286-MP-NOR-65D. 97–NARA 286-MP-TUR-171. 98–NARA 286-MP-GER-2035, U.S. Information Agency. 99–NARA 286-MP-UK-414, NARA 286-MP-GER-1700. 104, 105–Agency for International Development. 106–NARA 286-MP-LUX-90. 107–NARA 306-NT-345-3, Library of Congress. 114, 115–NARA 286-MP-YUG-237. 116–NARA 286-MP-GER-1769, NARA 286-MP-GER-1770, NARA 286-MP-GER-1772. 117–Agency for International Development, NARA 286-MP-GREE-1961. 118–NARA 286-MP-GER-938, NARA 286-MP-GER-939. 119–NARA 286-MP-GER-914, NARA 286-MP-GER-915. 124, 125–NARA 286-MP-GER-2002.